EZQUERRA

Lejanista Architecture

THE FREEDOM OF CREATION

ARCHITECT EZQUERRA with his team at his studio in Mexico City:

From left to right

Above:
Gonzalo Reza, Eduardo Velázquez, Pedro Ezquerra, Elia Ferrer, Fernando Herrera, Carlos Juárez, Gabriel Téllez.

Below:
Rodrigo Reyes, José Luis Ezquerra Jr., José Luis Ezquerra de la Colina, Arturo Calderón.

PHOTOGRAPHY: Pedro Ezquerra Borobia
Hans Rothlisberger
SKETCHES: José Luis Ezquerra de la Colina
TRANSLATION: Glenn R. Gardner
María Teresa Tracey
DESIGN: CENTAURIA CONSULTORES EN DISEÑO
EDITION: CORPORACIÓN EDITORIAL MEXICANA

Edited by
Coedi Mex, S.A. de C.V.
Av. Chapultepec No. 417 A, Desp. 5
Col. Juárez
México, D.F., C.P. 06600
E-mail: coedimex@df1.telmex.net.mx
Tel.-Fax. (5) 207-9991, (5) 207-9532
Registro Cámara Nacional de la Industria Editorial Mexicana núm. 3069

Editorial Director
Guillermo Pérez M.

Control and Organization
María Elena Trujillo S.

Author
José Luis Ezquerra de la Colina

Photography
Pedro Ezquerra Borobia
Hans Rothlisberger

Sketches
José Luis Ezquerra de la Colina

Editorial Design
Centauria Consultores en Diseño, S.C.
Bahía de Todos los Santos #40 –2
Col. Verónica Anzures
México, D.F., C.P. 11300
E-mail: centauria@excite.com
Tel. (5) 545-0369, (5) 254-2782
Tel.-Fax (5) 203-6309

Editorial Supervisor
Rubén Hernández

Editorial Control
Pro Imagen Editores
Córdoba, Argentina

Design Consultants
Juan M. Bruera
Silvia I. Oshiro

Supervised by
Alejandro Christe

Printed in Singapore by
Provision Pte. Ltd.
34, Wilkie Road
Tel. 65-334-7720
Fax. 65-334-7721

Production
Alice Goh

Translated by
Glenn R. Gardner
María Teresa Tracey

ISBN 968–5152–02–0

1st. Edition 2000
10,000 copies

CONTENTS

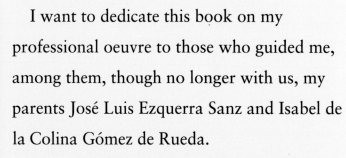

DEDICATIONS

I want to dedicate this book on my professional oeuvre to those who guided me, among them, though no longer with us, my parents José Luis Ezquerra Sanz and Isabel de la Colina Gómez de Rueda.

To my loving wife and companion, Josse Borobia y Souza.

To my children: Maribel and José Luis, Victoria and Miguel, María Pía and Francisco, María Luz and Iñaki, Iñigo Pedro and Juan Carlos.

As well as to the grandchildren already with us: Miguel, Francisco and Victoria Lascurain; María Pía, María Isabel and Ana María Fernández; Santiago and Paula Ezquerra.

...and to all those yet to come.

My thanks to the Universidad Popular Autónoma del Estado de Puebla (UPAEP) for their generosity, having believed in me and in my work, first publishing the book *Ezquerra y la arquitectura lejanista* in 1993.

José Luis Ezquerra de la Colina

To speak of the thought and oeuvre of José Luis Ezquerra de la Colina is only comprehensible in the coincidence of a singular institution of higher learning with a unique model of social solidarity in the country, in an encounter favoring the development of a Faculty of Architecture and blending the profile of the architecture and the author.

The founding of the Universidad Popular Autónoma del Estado de Puebla (UPAEP) is due to the urgent need to offer a possibility of higher education for the preservation of the human and national values of our culture vis-à-vis a stage of crisis and loss of direction in the present-day teaching of architecture and of urbanism.

The Faculty of Architecture, as founding body, is making an intense campaign to capture "nostalgic" concerns in the recovery of our national identity in architecture. That is how, in 1974, José Luis Ezquerra came to share his thought with students in his conference on "Educational Foundation of Shapes and Spaces," putting forth the postulate: "Spaces educate."

The presence of Ezquerra marks the first precedent in the schools of the country. Since that time, the most preeminent Mexican architects have passed through the "Architectural Weeks" of the UPAEP.

The theme of the "Architectural Weeks" dealt with the problems of the architect with a profile of humanism and cultural recovery that first crystallized in the principles underlying the school and, subsequently, with the "Movement of Re-encounter with Architecture" in 1983. Ezquerra, who had always been present, no longer was the same. His thought and his way of looking at architecture had evolved. Attempts were made to put Mexican architecture back on track, vis-à-vis the heritage from functionalism and internationalism. Along with the figure of Ignacio Díaz Morales, he marked the definitive guiding light of the "re-encounters with architecture" in Puebla.

We should mention that, on November 26, 1993, the Universidad Popular Autónoma del Estado de Puebla awarded the first "Ignacio Díaz Morales" National Prize for Architecture to architect José Luis Ezquerra de la Colina.

This is the singular and transcendental way Ezquerra makes academism, managing to germinate the seed of his thought in fertile soil. As he transforms ideas into shapes and spaces, he also conquers the spirit of the students and forms a school seeking to blend tradition with contemporaneity: nova et vetera.

It is undeniable that the creative spirit of José Luis Ezquerra de la Colina has been guided since that time by his *lejanismo* (cultural emotions and passions from the far-off past), nostalgia and burden caused by the memory of something lost. The "emotional burden of lost art" becomes a search for lost art, just as felt by Ruskin, Morris and others.

His personal stamp is laden with signs, shapes and abstractions inherited from his Hispanic origin with a Mediterranean-Mudejar flavor, expressed in a plasticism reflecting baroque sensuality. His life as a Poblano leaves the mark of the Mexican natural and cultural surroundings. From the hand of the artisan, from the freedom of shapes linking Man and Nature together in a cultural treasure made into stone and clay. It produces a synthesis of integrated forms, born of a blending: a happy encounter of two worlds.

FERNANDO RODRÍGUEZ CONCHA
Director, School of Architecture
Universidad Popular Autónoma del Estado de Puebla

PROLOGUE

TRADITIONS INTERWOVEN WITH MODERNITY

Louise Noelle

In approaching the work of an architect, it is always elucidating to seek to analyze him within the context of his time and his place, at the same time as studying his work and projects in particular. Only through the lens that gives value to the site and its conditioning factors, both geographic and cultural, is it possible to understand, in all its value, the full meaning of an architectural expression.

As such, in the development of present-day Mexican architecture, it is possible to point out how diverse trends have been formed starting in the sixties. Three of them correspond to a generalized wish to contribute new proposals vis-à-vis the international currents that still exist. It is a question of searches both in the formal field as well as in the recovery of elements such as patios and porticos in constructions where the wall predominates over the holes, without forgetting an approximation to certain traditional constructive systems. Therefore, faced with the vanguards from afar, sculptoric architecture and integral functionalism have been defined, as well as the prolongation of emotional architecture, derived from the pioneering proposals of Luis Barragán since the forties.

Within this latter trend falls José Luis Ezquerra, who shares with it the express desire to seek the emotional nature of spaces in his work. From this posture derive the eloquence of the sites, the plasticity of the buildings, the sensualism of the shapes, the whiteness of the walls, the mystery of the plazas and corner nooks, like a rejection of the coldness of the vanguards from abroad. In his case, he contributes cultural reminiscences, both local as well as Mediterranean.

It would be appropriate to point out here that, in present-day architecture, faced with the exacerbated posture of the contemporary movement and the doubtful responses of post-modernity, a considerable number of architects have drawn closer to regionalism as an honest response to the peremptory demands of new architectural solutions. This current seeks to resolve the debate and the antagonism between an impersonal and standardized architecture, of an international cut, and that which seeks, in what is local, the answers to the specific problems of economy, culture and environs, among others. Moreover, it constitutes a movement that proposes, in a

Sketch based on a Benozzo Gozzoli painting.
J. L. Ezquerra

sensitive and creative way, different options for the architecture of each site, without forgetting the postulates still lingering of the contemporary architecture which surfaced at the beginning of the twentieth century.

In this sense, Ezquerra himself became part of the regionalist movement in a quite particular way. With his *lejanista* position, this architect does not take the constructive and cultural antecedents of the site too rigorously into account, but rather approaches it under the point of view of history and the cultural relationships of sites far-off in space, but close in spirit. In addition, the strength of the walls, the dosage of openings and the artisan work in the constructions all aid in the same direction, without forgetting a careful and respectful insertion in the surroundings and the significant presence of vegetation and water, with the adequate and suggestive incidence of light.

So that, down through the years, he has fashioned a distinctive style that was inaugurated in the first projects of 1964 for the Las Hadas hotel in Manzanillo, a pioneer in many senses. It is a unique complex, where towers and minarets, vaults and cupolas, scrolls and cantilevers reign, which, blending with the vegetation and the whiteness of the walls, asserts itself vis-à-vis the powerful Pacific Ocean with the personal vision of his architecture. It is not a case of a simple adding of striking and innovative shapes, or of a scenographic complex. It constitutes the birth of a particular way of leisurely living on the oceanfront. This publication bears witness to his abundant later work, ranging from private residences to full-fledged hotel and housing complexes. Moreover, the rigorous discipline of the designer and the depth of his theoretical and spiritual concepts are set down.

With his constructions, this architect introduces us to the thinking of other times and other places, without forgetting the present and the particular conditioning factors of each project, so as to offer a masterful lesson of history and design. Time and space, reality and dreams, the rational and the exuberant, the Islamic and the Latin, the religious and the sensual, technique and imagination, materials and beliefs make up the different elements of a present-day alchemy capable of producing comfort, emotion and poetry, which are an integral part of José Luis Ezquerra's architecture.

Sketch of the Bosphorus, Istanbul.
J.L. Ezquerra

LEJANISMO

Introduction to Lejanista Theory

Drawing by J.L. Ezquerra Borobia

The Tree of My Beleifs

I believe in God,
That is why I proclaim sublime
faith and inspiration

I believe in the Trinity,
That is why I like geometry and
the order of Bernard de
Clairvaux, Palladio and Gaudi

I believe in the Spirit,
That is why I am filled with
enthusiasm by the passionate
Baroque light at Tonantzintla,
El Pocito and Rosary Chapel.*

I believe in Light,
that is why I use white, which
is the luminous synthesis of
the spectrum expressed in
Monet, Sorolla and Vasarely

I believe in the Creation,
That is why I am impassioned
by the possibility to recreate it
shown in the freedom of
Respighi, Vivaldi and Debussy

I believe in Man,
That is why I am reflected in
the historical emotion of Mont
Saint Michel, Dubrovnik and
the Alhambra.

I believe in Illusion,
Because, since it is not pure
reality, it allows me to work
with the dreams and utopias of
García Lorca, Joaquin di Fiore
and Don Quijote

I believe in Architecture,
to which I have dedicated my
whole life, with a profound and
certain vocation and of which
I believe that:

For all these reasons, it is and
must continue to be a sublime
expression of love!

JOSÉ LUIS EZQUERRA DE LA COLINA

* Tonantzinla: chapel in Cholula, Mexico
El Pocito: small church in the Villa de Guadalupe, Mexico City
Rosary Chapel: chapel in Puebla, Mexico

LEJANISMO

Architecture in Freedom

- *Background*
- *Evolution*
- *Four Pillars of Architecture and Urbanism*

Lejanismo

Time and Space
from a remote Distance.

The appearance of Architecture
–seen– from a distance
in time and space.

Salvation of Lost Traditions
of the past, incorporated
into the present
in physical form
through Architecture.

Architecture,
>   *"The Vocation of my Life"*

by José Luis Ezquerra de la Colina

La Ecología, painting by J.L. Ezquerra

To say *lejanismo* is Mexican architecture would be a bold and daring statement.

It is, in a way, reminiscent of the sixteenth-century religious buildings in Mexico, as in Huejotzingo and Santa María Tonantzintla, Puebla. These religious abodes were built by the indigenous people of Mexico, but, architecturally, they are expressions of Arabic and Spanish construction, developed with elements of design, identified today as Mudejar.

Lejanismo is a plastic necessity, an independent expression of architecture defined by critics as regional architecture and, more intimately, as emotional architecture.

Distant and remote architecture seen from distant imagery perceived by memories and imagination.

These visions of remoteness are not exact images, as those produced by a photograph or even by archaeology. The mathematical exactness of a form is not there, the contemplation is not a formalist vision of architecture. That would become a sad regression to the past.

We as architects have to have special ways of "seeing." It is essential to develop a vision which is not overpowered by rationality, because that would be Rationalism.

It is easier, then, to materialize our feelings, our emotions and the nostalgia into spaces and forms of the past brought to the present, salvaging, in a way, lost traditions of profound cultural image and unexplored memories.

My architecture is not Mexican architecture in and of itself. It can develop Mexican, or any other expression of the art in building. It might be Spanish, English, Peruvian, Moroccan, Mudejar, even Japanese or Chinese architectures.

That my spirit and aesthetic values envelop a Mexican soul, yes, they do, within the wide rivers of cultural breeding developed in Mexico between the diverse Mesoamerican cultures, Spain and the Arab world.

I have been very fortunate to live and work in Mexico, where I have enjoyed freedom of thought and of movement, which has allowed me to express myself through architecture.

While I was born in Spain, Mexico is, today, and has been my homeland and my nation, because it is also the home and country

Jósse Borobia, painting by J.L. Ezquerra

of one of the lines my forbearers established. Here a family, with my lovely and saintly wife, Josse. Together, we labored to give our children education, home and strong foundations based on our faith in God. One of them, the oldest, Pepe is an architect, like myself. I have been blessed by God with this family and with my work.

Louise Noelle, excellent friend and critic of architecture is actually the one responsible for the name *lejanista*, as I will describe later. Lejanista architecture derives from an internal process capable of producing, by emotion, images conducive to diverse forms of architecture and other expressions of art.

Brancusi is an excellent example of nostalgia. His sculptures speak about history, art and emotion. There is no doubt in my mind that. at the moment Brancusi produced his sculptures, he was in contemplation with an artistic - historical emotion, in nostalgia with Sumer Akkad. Conscientiously, he brought, into the present, forms from the past third or fourth millennium BC, which were the sources of his inspiration.

André Malraux makes an interesting description of this process. Brancusi was not in contemplation as an archeologist, archaeologer or as a *ristabilitore* of antiques.

To me, Brancusi adhered to the principles of *lejanismo*, extracting images from the past into the present. His taste for the history of Sumerian culture, his empathy and his emotions, dressed him with distant and remote feelings, without linking himself to his Western traditions. Together, they produced his art in sculpture.

Sumerian sculpture

I feel the same process happened within Picasso, Braque and Chagall. Proust remembers "the smell of wax on the wooden floors" of his home in youth. "The soft sensual and quivering feelings in the palm of his hand at the contact with the lustrous banister of the staircase" in his parent's home.

These emotions are expressed in his book: *La forme que j'avais pressentie autrefois et qui nous reste habituelle invisible cele du temps.*

The human spirit expressing itself in art is enormous unending and it would be foolish to assume that "modern life" was born but a century ago.

Solitude entices allurement, the charm and fascination of finding ones self. By loneliness an isolation, I found my real self. I was able

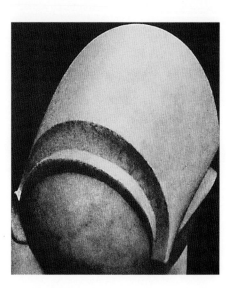

Brancusi sculpture

to speak with my own self. I was sweetly driven to the path of my emotions, to the sweetest and most delicate fibers within my soul. My spirit, then, with my nostalgia and my memories, directed me to my practice of art in architecture today.

EZQUERRA'S PHILOSOPHY

DREAMS

The love of history forced my spirit into action, making it flow along wonderful and marvelous creative paths.

One morning, I woke up with images of a pleasant dream: "sitting at the edge of a beautiful creek, there were two individuals, one a very serious and thoughtful man, the other was me." "Water, always water," said the man, "but never the same."

REALITY

That morning at my house, I met a mason by the name of Heraclito, who was to do some pending work. His name was imprinted firmly in my memory.

One evening, while reading Plato, I ran across Heraclitus of Ephesus. To my surprise, the page read as follows:

"Upon those who step into the same rivers, different and ever different waters flow down." The dream and these words were to become a philosophy for work. Plato's own thinking: "all things are in constant flux, however, often escaping our senses." "Mountains and rocks are temporarily stable, though they too will eventually change."

THE PARADIGM

My own life is paradigmatic of dreams and reality, of time and space.

In 1960, following a seminar on the "History of Architecture" and the exhibit "Art of Egypt," I traveled to Egypt.

EGYPT – MEDITERRANEAN

These days were the time of my studies at the National School of Architecture in Mexico. Professor and architect Agustín Piña Dreinhofer was in charge of the seminar and the exhibit.

This trip was a formidable encounter between history and my

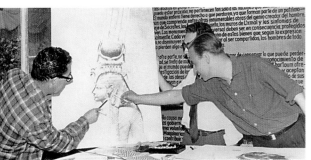

Architects Agustín Piña D. and J.L. Ezquerra setting up the "Art of Egypt" exhibit

work. This vital force led me to also formidable monuments, to ancient times, relics and symbols, monumental Nubian statues, Islamic architecture, Greek art from Byzantium, monasteries, gusty winds, drawing and misty seas, islands (Corfu) covered with cypress and olive orchids, a combination of strong emotions.

The Turkey of Ottoman, the incredible architecture of Sinan Abdulmenan, and Ibn Zamrack, the poet of the Alhambra.

All of this produced within me a hallucination beyond expectation. This, and my dreams as a child, developed my philosophy of architecture and my Decalogue of Design, ten guidelines, a natural system for me as an architect: My Ten Commandments

Sketch of Sinan Ibn Abdul Menan
J.L. Ezquerra

1. Skylines
2. Ensembles
3. Towers
4. Stairways
5. Roofs
6. Walkways
7. Water
8. Gardens
9. Patios
10. Doors

However

Nothing subcedes without effort and work. Comprehension and understanding is a process of the wind and of the spirit, and this is how we arrive at an understanding of culture. Had it not happened as it did, it is very probable that my attitude of "de-rationalism" would have merely been "metaphor."

Sometime in Paris, I heard these illuminating words: "Man has an enormous need for sweetness, sweet architecture for man's dimension, simply sweet and human, without mannerism or brutalization." Later, in Port Grimaud (southern France), I learned these words belong to architect Francois Sperry, once also a victim of Le Corbusier's dictatorship.

Surrealism and Lejanismo
A different attitude, contemplation of the past with nostalgia.

Remedios Varo

El Neoplatónico, painting by J.L. Ezquerra

Marcel Proust, James Joyce, Ruskin and Morris, Brancusi, Chagall, Picasso and Braque, Remedios Varo, poets and artists, in their own way and time, in their own space, have entered into a contemplation of the past, with nostalgia.

Lejanismo is an attitude of the soul, an expression of our feelings. Our cultural emotions release in complete and vital freedom.

If I had to define myself as a person, however, it would be difficult. However, I can define my architecture. It is consummated work, with a physical presence. It exists in this dimension which I today portray not only in this book, but, out there, standing up in each geographical parameter.

It is lejanista architecture, a surrealist expression of my feelings, my nostalgia, my distant cultural emotions, Eastern and Western manifestations, assimilated through almost forty years of uninterrupted architectural work.

THE FOUR PILLARS OF MY ARCHITECTURE
AESTHETICS AND METAPHYSICS OF PALLADIO – PLATO
PHILOSOPHIES OF GAUDI – CLAIRVAUX

Andrea Palladio, Antonio Gaudi, Plato and Bernard de Fontaines (Clairvaux) are cultural symbols of the four pillars of lejanismo.

With spirit and mind open, through the intellectual incursions of pensiveness, I discovered the masters of my thinking. "With them, and within them" a vision of the four pillars of architecture and urbanism appeared in my inner eye:

1. CREATIVITY
2. TRADITION
3. EXACTNESS
4. SPLENDOR

This vision confirmed my belief in Platoism, teaching us that "actual things are copies of transcendent ideas, and that these ideas are the objects of the knowledge apprehended by reminiscence."

LOOMING IN THE DISTANCE

Lejanismo can do no more than to loom in the distance, daring to interpret these transcendent ideas through reminiscence.

I would come to believe and understand that these are a matter of emotional conjectures, surmises of feelings and passions, reflections, congenialities and affinities which lead us to steer, in a different manner, the practice of architecture, thereby allowing our affections, our fondness and sympathy to flow like the water of a river into forms and functions.

A short review, in retrospect, the "recollections of my mind."

The study of history and the practice of emotion towards art "opened up my intellect," providing me with the creative freedom which I enjoy today.

There was something inside, forcing me to "free myself" from ignorance, to break away. I gained that freedom by refusing to follow the "ghosts" of the past, heading for a safe haven in the passion of my recollections.

I finally arrived at an understanding that "there is only one master to serve." Simplistic geometrics and rigid sketching had produced only boredom in me. Rigidity in sketching and sickeningly simple geometrics led me to radical decisions in my design: "I liberated myself from the chains in mind and hands." I was free! Come to think of this process, I think it was more the plastic pressure of circumstance, an urgency to express myself through drawing, the pleasures in searching and finding unexplored forms, spaces and times.

No doubt in my mind. I was beginning to understand the memories, objects, books, paintings and furnishings, furniture that in my infancy and youth I had seen and felt day after day in my parent's home. In a certain way, these recollections were "new discoveries," each discovery with its own value, lost conventions, practices and beliefs, the "lost orthodoxy" so expertly explained by Chesterton.

José Luis Ezquerra and his wife Josse in front of Ramses II, colossus at Abu-Simbel, Egypt, February 1961

The birth of the Lejanista concept

Mexican architecture "Archi-dialogues" at the "Architecture Society of the IPN" (National Polytechnic Institute), Mexico City, August 19, 1991.

Louise Noelle, academician, researcher, critic, in love with architecture, defined the philosophy of my architecture as "lejanista" that evening. From that day on, I have adhered to this term.

Conversations

Louise Noelle and I had many and diverse conversations about the theory of art and architecture, especially because she and her husband, Ruben Mereles, asked me to design and build a house for them on the

Sketch of Abu-Simbel, Egypt. J.L. Ezquerra

beach at Nuevo Vallarta, Mexico (Pacific Coast). This led to friendship and pleasant communications.

Don Juan de la Encina and Doña Pilar Zubiaurre

In those days, very pleasant meetings derived from the seminars given by Ricardo Gutiérrez Abascal, best known as "Don Juan de la Encina." He spoke to us in his pausing, Castillian accent about the baroque, style and space. Tranquil nights around the big "round table" of his home filled us with enthusiasm about the "Theory of Pure Visuality" and comments on "Invariants of Chueca Goitia," which created in me such a strong impression thereafter.

Doña Pilar Zubiaurre, his gracious wife, in delicate and gentle manners, supplied us with coffee and cookies, always there in the room. An atmosphere of a room full of objects and paintings. What stands out in my memory are those signed by her famous brothers, Los Zubiaurre, who were hearing impared. All of those who had the opportunity of being there amongst them felt the emotion for art, with great respect and interest for its history.

1991 Conference

In the later part of 1991, I was invited by the University of the Americas and the Universidad Popular Autónoma del Estado de Puebla in Mexico to give a lecture on occasion of the "Architectural Weeks." That was the first time I spoke informally about lejanista architecture, mounting a small exhibit. Earlier, I had lectured and given various conferences in academic circles about my architecture.

Discovering Mexico and me in Mexico

All of the experience gained and the external visions acquired gave me the insight to better understand and love Mexico and its extraordinary cultural past.

Those unforgettable months in the search of art, filled with emotions, never-ending images, transformed me in unusual ways. I could have not returned, even if I had tried, from where I went, being the same man.

My interest in the past of Mexico was greater and more refined than ever. I was never to separate myself from the Mudejar and Baroque past of Mexico.

Sketch of Saint Bernard de Clairvaux. J.L. Ezquerra

My Ten Commandments
DECALOGUE OF DESIGN

The basis of all great architecture is the harmonious arrangement of planes, surfaces, spaces and their intersections

I. Skylines

The horizon must produce equilibrium, harmonizing Heaven and Earth into one organic conjugal whole. If not, we do violence to nature which is created by God – and "God is the light of Heaven and Earth"

It is Unity of "Hansa" (hand of Fatima)
It is the Unity of Plato
It is the Unity of Bernard

II. Ensembles

Unity in diversity, if their celestial profiles harmonize with the skyline, their terrestrial forms will concord with the land, they will be in order with their natural surroundings. Harmony between vertical and horizontal lines gives both balance and diversity. Thus, spatial forms may be both varied and interrupted and, with equilibrium, multiple diversities may be achieved within one unified whole

"All which speaks of absolute unitarianism is dictatorship, just as all which is absolutely diverse is anarchy." Neither of these positions is desirable for the body and soul of Man, much less, desirable to God.

III. Towers

In their verticality, we are reminded of the mystical relationship between Man and his Creator. They are elements which identify places and cultures: symbols of reference.

"Magic mountains penetrating the heavens, sometimes lost among the clouds." Beacons resplendent to the spirit of Man.

They compensate and balance proportions and harmonize groups of buildings

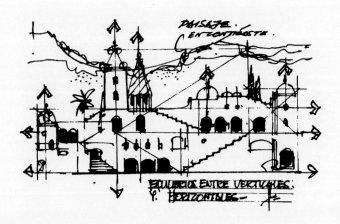

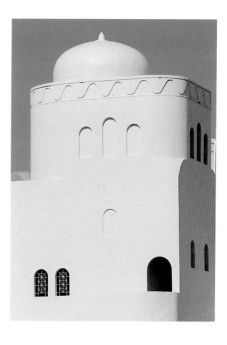

IV. STAIRWAYS

Spirals, pyramids, dreams of Jacob, fanciful
games, luminous receptors of Sun and Moon.
These ladders, stairs, steps lead the soul
through different emotional states, through
places of magic and mystery. They are flights
of fancy, escapes and escapades. The great
opportunity of architects and artists. The ups
and downs of life. The solution to vertical
lines

Coixtlahuaca.
Convento . Siglo XVI.
OAXACA.
MEXICO. 1990.

* Del libro. estudio.
OAXACA "Analisis del Ambito Construido"

v. ROOFS

We have called them the fifth façade because
they belong to the Moon, the Sun and the Air.
Those which no one wants to see, but are seen.
They shelter and dignify at the same time.
   They are the consummation of buildings
which lend personality and presence to each
body, like heads on mortal beings

"I saw the horizon,
   with its confusion of mists,
vapors and winds.
Towards heat and animals
that cried out on every side.
But I realized I had reached
the fifth façade and I saw
everything more clearly."

VI. WALKWAYS

Human communication. They appear in all colors, sizes and forms. They are petrified serpents with diverse and variegated scales.

Some can be walked slowly and barefoot. Others need hobnailed boots or rubber-soled sandals. There are many paths, not all are pleasing, but they have to be trodden.

Our art can be exalted by them, if they are expressed as carpets with undulating or geometric designs for the sweet and sensual walk between shadows and aromatic breezes, as if expecting, finally, to encounter Paradise

Machado wrote:
"Wayfarer, there is no way,
it is made on the way."
I believe Machado is
somewhat mistaken.
There are paths already made
by others, tragic or sweet,
and the wayfarer may
tread them all.

VII. WATER

It is light! And before the sea of salt and corals, or if coming from fountains, as in a fresh spring, it should embrace and envelop the architecture -be an integral part of it- refreshing its spaces and forms. The architecture should find its own reflection within it, confusing the real with the unreal.

Liquid silver running between jewels, which has no similarity, because of its transparency and purity.

"Confounding the sight with liquid and solid, water and marble and we know not which of the two is." Static or in motion.

This is how it was conceived by the poet and hydrologist of the Alhambra, in the time of Mohammed V, Ibn Zamrack

Water is the silvery liquid running in between the jewels with unparalleled beauty, because of its whiteness and transparency in the seas, in coral reefs along with salt, embracing beauty and life.

*Ibn Zamrack. Poet of the Alhambra.

VIII. GARDENS

The refined language of nature.
"Garden – I am that which by beauty is
adorned."
"Never was seen a more flourishing garden
    with so sweet and aromatic harvest."
                        Ibn Zamrack
                        Poet of the Alhambra

"Who showed you, my God, how to make
flowers
    and in one full-woven leaf, embroider loops
    in four or six travails?"
                        Soto de Rojas
                        from the poem:
                        "Paradise close to many
                        gardens open to the few"
                        1652

"Houses are gardens and gardens are houses"
    Some gardens are intimately connected
with water, which is the noblest part of the
garden, the most precious and desirable to
man, because it is the best proof that Paradise
exists.
                        Ibn Zamrack
                        Poet of the Alhambra

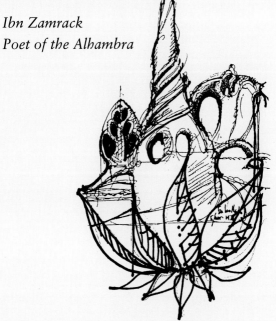

IX. PATIOS

Intimacy, fantasy, serenity, comfort and tranquillity.

Birds singing, the sound of water and scent of flowers. Could a space like this be created whose vapors would soothe my soul and relieve my sorrow?

Find architects who will contrive these corners of enchantment, no matter how large or small they be, cozy spaces where mortal Man will have the sky for a roof and fulfill his need for privacy away from the clamorous din which is disorder and anarchy

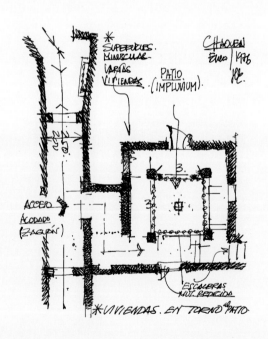

x. Doors

They are boundaries separating us from the outside world. Divisions which limit spaces and which intertwine through doors with a semblance of windows, architectural elements with infinite possibilities, infinite mysteries.

They can be great, almost monumental, medium-sized or small, to be cherished.

Doors for doves and storks, doors for dogs and cats, shutters through which pass sustenance or strains of troubadours.

Doors of terror which lead to infernos and those, radiant with light, which are opened by angels.

To where do doors lead?

From a medieval poem

Drawings by Ferdinand Bac

SELECTED WORKS

HOTEL
Las Hadas
MANZANILLO, COLIMA   1964 -1974

Las Hadas was born out of the romantic idea of two spirits and their imagination, those of Don Antenor Patiño and Doña Beatriz. Their dreams and my own took physical reality in Las Hadas. Today, an international tourist resort, considered one of the best hotels in the world during its peak of existence.

Las Hadas is part of a wonderful, magical and very human story. Here, one enters into a magic world of dreams, where time stops under intense blue skies in a mountain of magic covered with white forms and spaces, made up of arches in the doorways and windows. Silent, intimate, luminous white towers with trails, paths, plazas and curving roads consisting of tapestries of clay, marble, stone, greenery and flowers.

Ten upright, vertical, standing towers are the key architectural elements of the overall composition of the ensemble. These are the *vigilantes*, solitary angels in a haven of dreams. The most symbolic and prominent is the Water Tower, located at the uppermost point of two slopes. It is an observatory looking down over two huge sea inlets of distant and profound horizons.

The Sun, Moon, Air and Light each have their own tower at Las Hadas, as do Santiago, Pájaros, Mina, Estaño and Trajana. These towers, and particularly the Water Tower, can be seen on clear days and nights from far out at sea.

All of the trails, interior streets, pathways, roads and plazas interconnect with the towers. Intermingling with the towers, endless white spaces, comfortable and intimate, extend themselves within the ensemble at different heights aon the hillside facing the ocean.

Atemporality and irreality have made Las Hadas their home. Drowsy white forms have made it their mission to keep time asleep. The luminosity and brightness instilled by the "brutally white finishes" create a special atmosphere for listening to Debussy, Respighi, Mozart or any of the classical masters of music.

Las Hadas is a string of sensual emotions (*lejanismo ensoñador*), reminiscent airs involving solitary landscapes and scenarios, a basking oasis providing relief from routine and exhaustion, memories of refreshing palaces and shelters, freshness for the soul, mind and body, replenishing energy for the spirit.

Above: The Patiños: Doña Beatriz and Don Antenor on their yacht, with Las Hadas in the background
Below: Doña Beatriz, Walter Rupprecht and the architect at the construction site

In a matter of seconds at Las Hadas, one can travel from the Greek Islands to Granada and Marrakech, from Algeria to the Far East, from Tunes to the Adriatic coast and the south of Portugal.

In the twinkle of an eye and in complete intimacy, these sojourns are a way of life at Las Hadas. Strolling along the *callejas* and *callejones*, *rincones* and *plazas*, sidepaths and backroads, narrow curving trails and pathways, dead-ends and forgotten corners. There, one can steal a kiss at the "Rincón del Beso" (Kissers Corner) or visit the "Perro que Sueña" (Sleeping Dog Corner), or head down pathways with names like "Callejón del Duende," "Santa Elena," "Santa Beatriz" and "María Cristina" or stroll along and enjoy plazas like "Don Simón" and "Doña Albina."

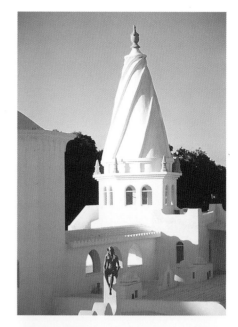

A mixture of cultures displayed at a seaside resort, the "Pueblo de Las Hadas." Mudejar style together with the ancestral cultures of the Americas, like the white town of Comala, "Pueblo Blanco de América" in the State of Colima.

Mudejar belfries and gables, XVI-century chapels bearing silent witness to the forms of the artistic expressions of Mexican craftsmen, world-renowned for their exquisiteness.

Las Hadas would not be what it is today without the able hands of the masons, masters in the art of vaulted chambers, cupolas and domes. The not only interpreted my designs with exactness, but even improved upon them.

This ornamental influence can be seen all over Mexico, particularly in the coastal areas, Oaxaca and Yucatán.

Edward A. Killingworth, president and CEO of Killingsworth, Stricker, Lindgren, Wilson & Associates, architects-designers of the Kahala Hilton in Honolulu, wrote me a very nice letter which I treasure as part of my personal files. It reads as follows:

> *"I don't know how to express*
> *my rejoicing with the beauty*
> *of this original creation...*
> *without a doubt, it is marvelous!*
> *Like an architect, I can understand*
> *what he created.*
> *It is a unique experience*
> *and you should be highly recognized.*
> *He is more than exceptional,*
> *I would say that he is a prodigy!"*

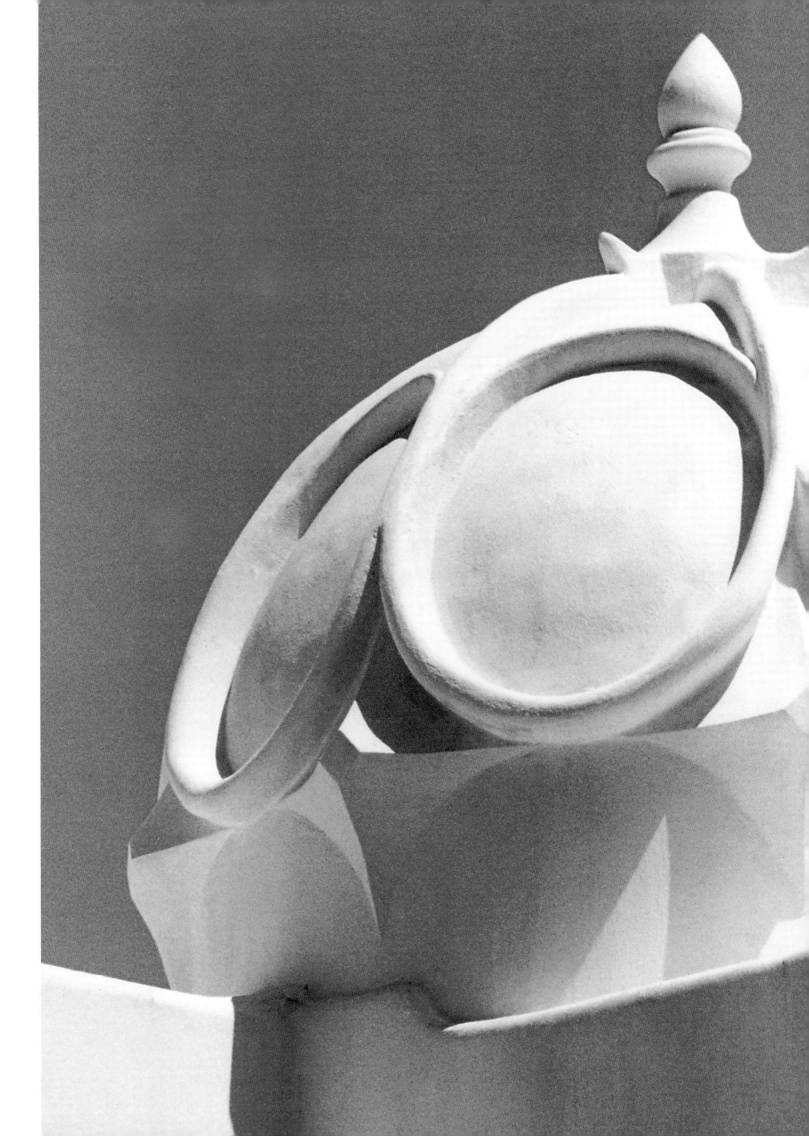

Don Antenor Patiño and Doña Beatriz

Antenor Patiño made it possible.

I am greatly indebted to Mr. Patiño. Las Hadas would not exist today without the character and the strong will of this man from Oruro, Bolivia. He inherited, I am sure, the stubbornness of his father, Don Simon Iturri Patiño, the man who built a mining empire in Bolivia out of tin.

A strong will and character are not divorced from feelings. Sometime before his passing away, with emotion, he shared with me his pride and and being moved when a young lift operator at the Pierre Hotel in New York complimented him on "the wonderful Mexican hotel he had made possible called Las Hadas."

A young man was expressing his admiration, not because he was a rich heir or was financially powerful, but, perhaps moved by the media, because Don Patiño had done something wonderful and valuable in Mexico.

Extraordinary Taste

Beatriz Patiño, "Doña Beatriz," showed remarkable taste in her suggestions for the original decoration of Las Hadas. Her guiding suggestions, carried out by Valerian Rybar, Jean Paul Olivier and Francois Catroux, adapted admirably to the basic spirit of the architecture. Together, we implemented a plastic integration beyond expectations. Originally, the rooms and suites had very simple and fresh tones, leaving the decor with a "good taste." I am sure, Beatriz will agree with me on this.

Hans Rothlisberger

Las Hadas has no better friend and supporter than my dear friend Hans. His love and passion for the resort and my work go beyond, sometimes, even myself. John Haase, also a good and dear friend, as well as Robin Leach, are the motors behind the enthusiastic friends of Las Hadas.

Thank you all, from the bottom of my heart.

Last, But Not Least, My Thanks to Many...

I would be committing an act of injustice if I purposely were to ignore the hands of hundreds, perhaps thousands, of Mexican artisans, masons and assistants who not only interpreted my designs exactly, but even improved on the forms and spaces contained in Las Hadas. The wonderful hands of men, and of unrelenting time.

Torre del Agua. Geometrical color
drawing by J.L. Ezquerra

Row of pigeon lofts. Geometrical
color drawing by J.L. Ezquerra

Aerial view of Las Hadas hotel
Photographer: John Frost

...And, of course I agreed.

This past May 31, at her home on Rue Murillo in Paris, Beatriz told me: "Antenor, everything he did, he did with a great deal of enthusiasm and illusion."

And as a sort of message, she made the following reflection, which she wanted to be published in my book:

"José Luis, all the love and illusions of those years to create a place of quality and of dignified beauty which we all shared and wished for Las Hadas. The efforts and enthusiasm that you and Luis* made together to achieve it cannot be left in oblivion. You all have to fight for Las Hadas to recover its place in beauty and prestige that it had internationally.

This would be the best memory and homage to our lives."

Beatriz Patiño
Paris, France

*Luis de Rivera

Club Maeva
MANZANILLO, COLIMA **1977 -1979**

Las Hadas became a trigger for tourism, investment and construction. The hotel filled to capacity as individuals as well as companies got wind of it and flocked into Manzanillo. It was on the scale of the California Gold Rush. Land ownership changed from hand to hand, real-estate speculation set in and construction took off at an unprecedented pace.

As result of this construction fever on Mexico's "New Riviera," I was appointed by Club Mediterranée (the operators) and Casolar (the owners) as their architect in charge of designing, developing and building 1,001 villas on a quite short strip of land, Las Peñitas, in front of the Bahía de Santiago. I was facing a dire situation. Problems are opportunities. I took the opportunity.

I spent days and nights sketching and drawing, thinking, researching and, then, the solution came to mind: Chechaouén at the rif, a Moroccan city in the North of Africa, a country of Tuaregs and Kabyles, the Chaounite Rockery.

The fortress city of Salé on the Atlantic Ocean, in front of Rabat and Chechaouén. This was the basis for my solution and proposal for my clients.

From that moment on, nothing stopped me, drawing and sketching, *al-koobas*, brackets and medallions, *at-twariqs* (capitals), ornamental Mudejar plasterwork, Berber elements, diverse stairway shapes, totally different from Western parameters.

In 1844, Charles de Foucauld wrote about the sacred city of Chechaouén and its great mosque, Ras-el-Ma, and the ten sacred sanctuaries with gardens and fountains, plazas, streets and minute homes and, yes, that is true, dimensions are tiny because the city sits on the steep rocks of a series of cliffs: Chechaouén ("Nine Horns" which, in reality, are two peaks in the village. No flat land is available, so that the builders of Chechaouén had to develop their streets and buildings in a very restricted and ingenious way).

Maeva's design was inspired in the solutions of the Islamic-Moroccan architecture of Chechaouén and its typical hamlets.

I was confronted with the problem of finding a proper and aesthetic arrangement of architectural elements. Fortunately for me, not on rought terrain like the chaounite rocky area, where rugged paths

Preliminary sketch by J.L. Ezquerra

Architect Ezquerra sketching in Chechaouén, Morocco

and plazas are practically "anchored" to the cliff. A crowded urban setting of very suggestive architectural spaces and volumes that served me well as inducements to sketch the master plan for Maeva.

I remember with delight the surprised faces of the engineers and technical staff pointing out the major mistakes I had made in my stair sketches. I had to introduce and explain to them the unheard of architectural specifications of Islamic architecture and, at the same time, make these terms familiar. Only then were we able to establish a common language that made possible a particular character in the architecture that to me is Mudejar.

The *al-kooba* is an extension of the bedroom. Originally, it was a bed closed by doors and shutters. However, at Maeva, I designed these alcoves at different levels and without doors, but with quite unorthodox, "fun" stairs accessing the bedroom. In the back of my mind was the thought that children would be the main users of these spaces.

Maeva is a modern version of Mexican Mudejar architecture and, I might add, the architecture of Mexico is, or was, Mudejar, to a good degree, until the baroque period and the end of Spanish colonial architecture.

Mexico today is a blend of cultures, a nation formed by very strong bloodlines from the Americas and Europe.

The crossbred style of Ibero-American architecture has been called "mestizo" by some, but I dislike this term because it implies superiority of one over the other. Therefore, I prefer *Mudejar architecture* much more, which is, after all, what the men from southern Spain brought with them to the Americas: the Muslim-Mudejar period of architecture, the Moorish style continued under Christian rule.

Mudejar is a combination of Spanish-Moorish elements, such as wooden ceilings in geometric patterns, colored tiles, rectangular archway frames (*alfices*) and the trefoil arch.

Native of the Americas enriched this beautiful architecture with their hands and their spirits, today spread all over Spanish America as witness to the union of cultures.

The welcome message of A.G. Sadek, Secretary of the Syndicate of Engineers, in Cairo in 1961, to a small group of Mexican architects (among them, myself) visiting Egypt, stated:

> *Gentlemen:*
> *"It is a pleasure to welcome you to Egypt. After all, you are not foreigners in the Arab world, since your ancestors originally came from Spain. Therefore, you should feel here as in your own home."*

Sierra Manzanillo
MANZANILLO, COLIMA **1986 -1990**

I believe that, in the future, the trend in new cities and, especially tourist ones, what we call ecotourism, should contemplate some humanized and balanced structures with regard to land, despite the the saturation.

The land, approximately 28,000 square meters of surface area, is located along the Audiencia beach, on the Santiago peninsula. It has a rough topography, with steep slopes, especially in the southern and western part.

We baptized different rooms of the public areas of the hotel with names such as *Los Navegantes*, *La Sierra*, *Las Audiencias* and *Los Tibores*, in reference to the *Nao de China* (China Galleon) and the Philippines. But in marked interest, we gave our public plaza a space–similar to the one we made at Las Hadas in homage to Doña Albina, mother of Antenor Patiño–geared to open-air banquets, concerts, exhibitions and plays. It is to be used for all types of outdoor activities in the late evening and early night, so pleasant and refreshing.

We wanted to dedicate this space to another woman forgotten by history. To a woman who was the victim of the fidelity that drove her to madness and the grave, victim of a passion for justice and the defense of the native peoples of the Americas, whom she protected from the Bourguignon pretenses of beloved son, Charles V, the emperor. In 1918, García Lorca wrote an elegy for this oft misunderstood queen, daughter of the great Isabel:

> Granada was your deathbed, Doña Juana,
> that of the old towers and the silent garden
> that of the dead ivy on the red walls
> that of the blue mist and the romantic myrtle.

There are many corners about which anecdotes could be written. For example, the shape and space of the La Hidra beach restaurant were inspired in this mythological and real being. The structure of the locale is based on the organic principle of this being, in its marine significance, a tube-like polyp closed on one end and with several tentacles on the other.

Preliminary sketch of tower
J.L. Ezquerra

Above: Sketch of the gallery,
Plaza de Doña Juana. J.L. Ezquerra
Below: Gallery, Plaza de Doña Juana

I cannot conclude without talking about the shape of the towers, which remind me medieval turrets and dungeons, of knightly dreams, of fairies and dragons. The shape of the building in different bodies was achieved with the whole of these towers and small windows, accentuating the moderating verticality. I made them round, because I identified more with the softness and static nature of cylinders, and white, because I consider that ivy, bougainvillea and myrtle should be growing on the voids.

The era and the supposed encounter on the Audiencia beach encouraged me to use the profile of XVI-century Isabeline and Mudejar arches. So that they are slightly pointed, not the Roman arch in Romantic style.

Suite interior

Panoramic view of hotel

Faldas de la
Alcazaba
BAJA CALIFORNIA   **1985 -1988**

The project is located at the tip of Baja California Sur, in San José del Cabo, forming part of a tourist corridor between San José del Cabo and Cabo San Lucas, right on the slopes of the Vigía hill.

Panoramic view of resort from golf course

It was proposed as part of the Image Master Plan to be adopted as the design norm and criterion for future projects in the area, in order to consolidate the distinctive image of the tourist pole in question, in both urban as well as architectural aspects.

Within the master plan, as a overall concept, two projects in particular were developed. The first, the clubhouse of the San José del Cabo golf course and, the second, the one called Faldas de la Alcazaba.

One of the elements underlying the project is the arch, which appears with variants like the Roman arch, and the three-point or *escarzano* arch. Massiveness predominates over voids, inclined coverings, cone-shaped accessways and windows, niches, latticework, columns, capitals, flying butresses or a splendid design for pavements and floors, be they indoor or outdoor.

The additional resources making up the whole are the pergolas, the ironwork, the masonry benches and low walls. Finishes and basic materials are rustic outside, semi-rustic inside, with rounded edges and painted a single color, as theme of the project. Outside, floors sport geometrical designs, using the river stones, flagstone and golden stone of the region. The washed and chiseled concrete form patterns and diagonal rain troughs which resolve the slopes of the pavement esthetically.

Very special and particular mention is to be made of the participation of architect Enrique Hernández Jaime of the Area of Planing of Fonatur, who was energetic in seeking the cultural identity of tourist developments in Mexico. Without his initiative, I do not know if San José del Cabo would have been better or worse, but certainly much different.

"One can conclude that the style proposed by Ezquerra, both in the original master plan as well as in the projects developed on those bases, especially for Faldas de la Alcazaba, brings together elements of our traditional Mudejar architecture and those of the vernacular. A new new harmony, typical of the area, was achieved, which served as a model for projects developed afterwards. This is how the style and image was created which conferred identity on the tourist development of San José del Cabo."

Architect Sergio Dominguez de la Sierra

Clubhouse

CLUB
Mediterranée
IXTAPA, GUERRERO **1979**

The spirit of the Club, despite its operational concepts, was closer to the creativity sought in the culture and tradition of the peoples. The project for Playa Quieta was tackled with this in mind. The first theme to be resolved was to create a pre-established system of circulations for the work that would not destroy the flora and fauna of the area. Once the pragmatic and logical form of the overall floor plan was resolved, very strict adaptations were made so as not to destroy areas which could not be substituted ecologically.

Happily, the piece of land was huge. It ran along the beach for almost a kilometer and was some 250 meters deep. The topography was rolling, that is, flat areas alternating with slopes and hillocks, making it possible to create a landscape all the more beautiful because of its variety.

The architecture we projected was quite simple, making use of local coastal characteristics, such as clay-tile floors and sloping red-tile roofs. Because of its simplicity, the buildings were the virtue, due to their location within the whole, being quite isolated and ending up generously covered by vegetation.

Panoramic view of Club

Villa Solaris
CANCUN, QUINTANA ROO 1985

Located on Kukulcán street between the Caribbean Sea and the Nichupté Lagoon, it has a very attractive location because of having two very valuable views: the sea and the lagoon.

The complex is white with sloping roofs covered with terra-cotta tiles. The volumetrics were inspired by the medieval complexes of the Adriatic, Dubrovnik in particular, with its solid masses built at different levels, granting it a sensation of strength and autonomy among the neighboring projects.

The very special distribution of St. Marks Square in Venice suggested the portico of the Plaza Porticada to me. The latter does not relate to the sea, as happens with the Venetian square, with the exception of one of its sides. Through a stairway at a 90° angle, we reach the open area of the swimming pool, which does indeed face the sea.

I have always thought it necessary to avoid the boredom produced by unitary spaces trying to be so obvious. Diverse spaces should be created that produce bursts of emotion and, why not, mystery!, in the onlooker. This can be experienced and felt in cities like Venice and Dubrovnik.

There is another place, unique and incredible, almost perfect, which I have never been able to free myself from wanting to emulate. It is the perfect triangle, the perfect "cosmic mountain," crowned by archangel St. Michael in the majestic spire of its marine mound, in the confines of Normandy: Mont Saint Michel. From this mound right in the middle of the sea and the sands comes, with true passion, a real delight for pinnacles and triangular formations. Whenever I can, I put them in my projects. Undoubtedly, I relate them in my subconscious with Trinitarian metaphysics and the order, likewise Trinitarian, of Palladio.

Preliminary sketch of interior plaza
J.L. Ezquerra

Kea Lani
MAUI, HAWAII   **1986 - 1992**

Maui is one of the eight islands of the Hawaiian archipelago. To the West and separated by three channels are the islands of Molokai, Lanai and Kahoolawa. In front of the latter, in the Alalakeiki channel, is the property where the Kea Lani hotel was projected, which means "white sky" in Hawaiian. It was inspired by one of the most typical flowers of the island: the white plume that grows next to the sea and, naturally, in the local architecture, distinguishes itself notably from the rest of the hotels in Hawaii.

It is true that Kea Lani is a son of Las Hadas. There are shapes used in the architectural-design process that are quasi-formal interpretations. However, I can say that they are a minimum part. On the contrary, the professional work of architect Francis Oda (Group 70 of Honolulu) was notable in the adaptation and solution of the style to the pragmatic, constructive and finishing realities of Hawaii.

In 1986, the conceptual design or pilot project was begun, for which it was necessary to travel to the islands to get to know them. It was evident that the clients were searching for our style and were convinced of it, but it had to be adapted to the systems and economy of the U.S. as well as justified culturally, rooting it in the Hawaiian idiosyncrasy. The latter turned out to be quite enrapturing and motivating.

The first thing recommended to us by Donald Graham—a well-established figure, in love with the islands since 1943, with an excellent library and a valuable source of information—was to visit the great artist Herb Kawainui Kane, author of a series of paintings *Travel: History of the Discovery of Hawaii*, which narrates the odyssey of the balsas from the Ra'iatea and Tahiti routes, and that of the Marquesas Islands in Polynesia. Herb Kane, as he is known, is the artist par excellence of Hawaii. A man of great stature, intelligent and universal, he has a generous Chinese inheritance from the Kanes and a island one from the Kawainui.

Preliminary sketch of main entrance and lobby. J.L. Ezquerra

On October 13, 1986, we spent a pleasant and fruitful day at his charming Kona plantation on the Big Island, from where one can see the historic coast where the battle between Kameamean and Captain James Cook took place, the latter loosing his life in 1779.

From him, we heard versions and legends supporting the theory of Mexican (New Spanish) origin in the discovery of Hawaii, such as that of navigator Juan Gaetano, who supposedly discovered them sailing between Mexico and the Philippines. It must have been one of the first trips after the return voyage of Antonio López de Legaspi and Andrés de Urdaneta, though there is little proof. However, Herb Kane has small figurines that were found by him on the eastern coast of the Big Island and that represent New Spanish-type individuals.

I should point out that, on the island of Maui, for example, there is an equestrian tradition quite similar to Mexican *charrería*. Besides, on these islands, cowboys use sombreros and bandanas in the style of northern Mexicans. They are called *paniolos*, quite close to the Spanish term by which they should have been called during nearly 300 years of New Spanish navigation, when the Manila or Acapulco galleons passed by or perhaps even moored on these coasts, both on the outward voyage, passing along the South, or on the return voyage, to the North of the archipelago.

In my search for roots, what I did was to culturally link Kea Lani with the architecture of the Royal Hawaiian Hotel, built in 1927 on Hispano-Mexican and native models, with quite surprising results. Today, it is the pride and heart of Waikiki and, of course, of Hawaii.

In the analysis of Hawaiian architecture, an important building is the Iolani Palace. Neo-classical and white, it was built in 1882 in Honolulu by King Kalakaua. Curiously, it is the only royal palace the U.S. has. In the same city, there are XIX century neo-classical banks, using themes and decorative elements quite typical of the flora and fauna of the islands on their façades. One could also take into account the architecture of the Catholic and Protestant missions of the XVII and XVIII centuries.

Before the evangelization of the islands, architecture was practically nil. Some acropolis remains, forts such as Kawaihge, totemic buildings such as tombs and temples, and a great wealth of palisades and floors richly decorated with dirt, stones and ephemeral flowers, are a sampling of the naturalist life practiced by their inhabitants.

Therefore, Kea Lani has quite valid and quite Hawaiian antecedents from the era of the monarchy, prior to the American boom.

Villa Loose
COYOACAN, MEXICO CITY 1961

"We find ourselves before a true work of present-day architecture, which we could signal as one of the first outcroppings...of a new style which, without totally breaking the course of functionalism-rationalism (there is still some hesitation, there is a lack of conscience of a language of its own), slants it, orients it toward greater freedom, where space and volume are not so rigid, so defined, so mechanical, where profit is not the maximum value, but the delight, the daydream, the sentiment and the emotion are taken into account and exhalted, occupying the proper place in our existence."

Architect J. José Reveles, Mexico, 1963
Associated with Klaus Feldman
Owners: Herman and Helma Loose

Upper and lower floors

Sketch of villa accessway
J.L.Ezquerra

Stained-glass window. Design by J.L. Ezquerra

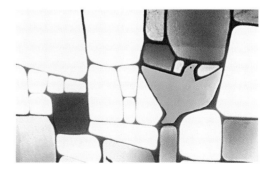

Villa Colomba
PEDREGAL, MEXICO CITY **1961**

When contemplating the plans drawn *ex profeso* for this publication, seeing the movement of lines and strokes regarding the voluptuosities of lava in the Pedregal de San Angel neighborhood, I deduce and can understand much better the decisive sentiments that led me to make precisely those strokes, and not others.

Preliminary sketch of interior
by J.L. Ezquerra

The forms of extraordinary protuberances and grotto-like holes, sinuous and undulating surfaces of petrified igneous crust, were the motives for inspiration or perhaps even respect...immense respect for them!

For some years of my career, I worked proudly with several architects of whom I harbor pleasant memories. One of them, Francisco Artigas, had taught us to "see the Pedregal" from his own perspective. His projects were rationalistic and modular, but they were imbued with excellent quality and finishes. Making an interesting conjunction of straight lines on white concrete and glass, they alighted gracefully, hardly touching, on the black baroque forms spewed up centuries before by the Huehueteotl mountain of the Xitle volcano.

However, fascination with shapes was to grant me the possibility of a different conception of the land I had right before my eyes. And so I came to a realization of the need to involve myself more in-depth with nature, so as to extract from it its reality and formal consequences.

For many different reasons, the house was never finished, remaining abandoned for many years.

Owner: Melchor Rodríguez Caballero

General floor plan

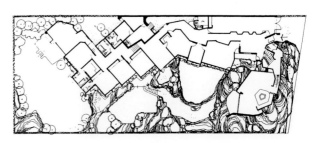

Villa Valladolid
MORELIA, MICHOACAN **1962**

With characteristics similar to Villa Loose, Millarca and Colomba, in this case, the lot was typically urban-residential, situated on a corner.

Therefore, the decision to make a side entrance provided the house with a particular interest and a volumetric mobility somewhat abstract, which permitted demonstrating the possibility of movement in the shapes, especially when combining the quarry stone and black volcanic rock with the white surfaces, in a curious symbiosis of creolization.

I would not venture to state that this had been the initial intention, not even that we were conscious of seeking cultural identification, an objective which, over time, would come to be considered something indispensable and unpostponable in the field of architecture.

What we can indeed say is that, unconsciously, we were practicing a burning desire to express ourselves that, as in the preceding cases, involved clear falterings and indefinitions.

That this past turned out to be history and now we understand it better. We can more clearly understand how, in its time, one could still perceive the enchantment with the shapes of formalist Le Corbusier, but, happily for us, already removed from pure rationalism.

Associated with architect Mario Guízar
Owner: Rosendo Sánchez Corona

Villa Millarca
CLUB DE GOLF LA HACIENDA, 1963 STATE OF MEXICO

In the periodical *Mañana* of December 28, 1963, Julio González Tejada, wrote:

"The only thing a wide-ranging group of young Mexican architects needs is that those who have the economic power to finance the raising of new buildings have confidence in them and, more than anything else, an interest in keeping people conscious that architecture is not just one of the most beautiful disciplines of art, but the most important one and, as such, should be taken into consideration and propitiated."

Julio González was speaking precisely of Villa Millarca, a project done at the request of the Salazar family, whom were defined as the owners and sponsors of an architecture representative of an era and of a generation or, at least, of a non-conformist trend.

It is true that, down through time, I was fortunate to have the trust (though at times I obtained it through a great deal of effort) of these "sponsors of architecture," clients being so important for us. Good work has to meet up with good clients. Knowing how to make them enthusiastic about architecture is something fundamental, which depends on us.

Associated with architect Horacio Hernández
Owners: Alejandro and Maye Salazar

Upper and lower floors

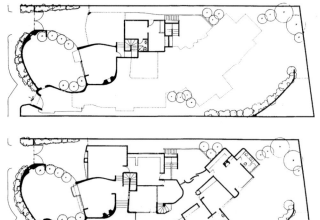

Villa La Atalaya
SANTIAGO, COLIMA **1977**

Situated on one of the most spectacular points of the Santiago peninsula, dominating Manzanillo Bay from its East-West position, because of its geographical location, it is an authentic *atalaya* or watchtower. On its eastern side, a spillway under the roofs of the port of Las Hadas and, on the western side, it rises up, doing justice to its name, on impressive cliffs, at whose base break the waves of the open sea.

The Atalaya is at the end of Rey Colimán street. Before entering the house, there is a polyhedral fore-patio of whitewashed walls that strain the breezes and permit framed views of the outside landscape. Walls are covered with climbing plants and a fountain-well with a curbstone in its center harmonizes with bunches of palm trees that refresh the area just before the house. To go from the fore-patio to the house, one crosses wrought-iron grillwork with tropical motifs.

My emotions in this project came from exuberant baroque shapes of tropical flora. I topped it off with stucco representing trays with flowers and fruit. The forged balcony railings and grillwork were designed as twisted plant stalks. We sought the integration of the air slithering over the surface of the walls, penetrating and uniting with the water.

Of course, a villa like this proved unusual and bare on the heights of a rocky crag. However, over time, I have enjoyed seeing how the vegetation has harmoniously crept over the architectural mass, softening it in the landscape. I have found this characteristic a constant in almost all my projects. It believe that, to a good measure, this is due to the fact that, in the original conception, I always took into account leaving spaces, so that vegetation would grow freely about the house, embracing it.

In the Atalaya, I forgot about cupolas, resolving the roof structures with sloping planes, with the enormous possibility of providing free ledges, since, with them, "one molds the profile of the sky," as Hassan Fathy would say.

Villa Coliman
SANTIAGO, COLIMA **1978**

A tower in the form of a needle at the entrance is the symbol of "La Punta," which goes well with the program of control, security and administration of the access building.

The design of Villas Coliman got its inspiration in the grain silos (*hórreos*) of northern Spain, elevated on four, six and eight rock pillars, like the *palaffittes* of the ancient lake dwellings built on piles. The purpose of the elevation was to avoid humidity and the plundering of predators. The idea seemed to me quite adaptable, because the pilasters would add to the swimming pool area and the terraces at this level, giving it an airy sensation of stability and elegance.

The roofs tended towards a four-sided pyramid covered by Spanish tiles. Surrounding the central constructed volume, a type of terraced porch-like walkway was designed.

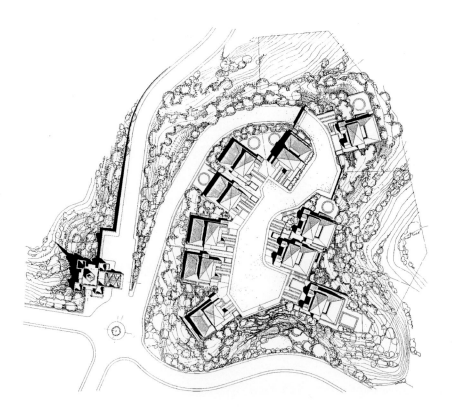

General floor plan.

Villa Coral
SANTIAGO, COLIMA 1979

The elements and influences reaching us from the sea are like a great desire of resurrection in the rendezvous with time and cosmos. They are like a symbiosis of all our thoughts and traditions. These thoughts were the ones inspiring me that day so I could order and plan the project.. I remember a conversation with Eugene Cernan, the astronaut, who was very enthusiastically involved with the project.

Happily, the owner shared these thoughts, which made possible his comprehension and support in carrying out the work just as we had proposed.

With the passage of time, I have been able analyze some laws which, over time, have become clear to me. In this case, I refer to some concepts on shapes, expressed in the "Manifesto de La Alhambra"—a document elaborated by a group of Spanish architects in the city of Granada in 1953—considering them applicable, though in small proportions and in different ways, to Villa Coral.

In Villa Coral, mass does not exist as an esthetic value, but it is volume that counts independently and autonomously, even though the interrelationship of the parts with the whole is sought and definitively obtained. So that the volumetric world is infinite and each shape has its autonomy, adapting itself rationally to the topography of the terrain.

Chueca Goitia used to say: "Recalling the profile of the Alhambra, as a whole it forms a convex space (walled-in hill), within which a series of architectural areas opens up according to the functions sought and gives rise to different milieus in which the construction rises, closing off spaces."

Of course, in contrast with the Alhambra, which is concave in its interior spaces (life inward, in idyllic conjunction with its gardens), Villa Coral should open up and depend on the formidable landscape surrounding it, like any project facing the sea.

The patio disappears as a secluded and concave element, becoming the (convex) center of the house (living room, dining room, music and game room, terrace and pool), from which the roofs of the six villa apartments open out like a fan. These were thought of as rock gardens, perhaps in the *lejanista* emotion of those of the Duke of Bomarzo in Tuscany. Only, in this case, instead of terrifying monsters, I fed imagination with huge crustaceans and conch shells, the size of Jules Verne's Nautilus, which are part of the "fun" by being able to walk on them and touch them with your bare hands and feet.

I have to confess that I have a special attraction for roofs, since I consider that, in places of craggy topography, they are one of the most important façades of the landscape, that is, the fifth façade, converting them thus in natural extensions of the gardens.

The Koran says: "If the garden is paradise, the house should come as close as possible to its appearance and be a paradise." So we can understand that: "the house is the garden and the garden the house" (verses of Ibn Zamrack, in the room of the Two Sisters in the Alhambra).

Preliminary sketch by J.L. Ezquerra

Villa Casarena
SANTIAGO, COLIMA **1979**

Villa Casarena is situated on very steep terrain, on the western slope of the Cerro Colimán. Its name derives from one of its most salient characteristics: it is a house covered with sand, indeed. The owners' requirement was quite clear. The house was to blend totally into the landscape.

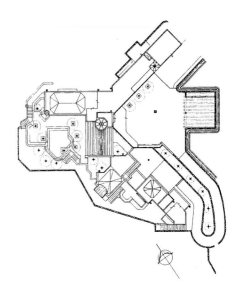

There were many and varied attempts to establish the color of the house, since it varied according to the luminosity of the sun, be it at dawn, full daylight or dusk. Finally, we thought that a natural color, not subject to paint formulas, would be obtained using sand from the nearby La Escondida beach. The advantages were that the color would remain stable and there would be material available for future maintenance. The idea was accepted and, based on resins and egg white, a coating was applied, achieving a result that was quite original and pleasing.

Cyclones and natural erosion require a certain maintenance that is done practically, using small amounts of sand from the beach, thereby avoiding the enormous difficulty represented by matching colors. Inside, color was used according to the decoration design planned for each space, though the decorative base of the color of sand was maintained.

Another of the project requirements set by the owners was regarding style. They own precious objects and collections of Oriental art, especially Indian. Their house is a palace of refined good taste, both because the atmosphere producing so many objects, as well as because of the lifestyle they have established.

Therefore, their vacation villa should be a continuation on the scale of the style to which they were accustomed. The *lejanismos* of India were fundamental elements in the project.

The third basic requirement was the scale of the house. It should almost be miniature, monastic and austere. In the process, the initial austerity gave way until obtaining spaces, though never exaggerated, very convertible and cozy indeed, virtues typical of the villa.

I cannot finish my chronicle on Villa Casarena without first making some comments about its interiors and decoration. Each wall was finished and resolved with stucco, arches and special friezes. Each one of the bathrooms had a solution based on tiles designed by us, fired in the Bajío region, and whose molds were destroyed so that no copy whatsoever existed, resulting in a very original decoration. The floor stones were brought from special calcareous sediment banks from the Atoyac River in Puebla.

It was a very complete and satisfactory experience, in which, at the unavoidable request of the owners, we were able obtain an architectural work that was exceedingly special and none too common. Villa Casarena was planed, built and decorated by our own organization. This allowed us to obtain very high quality, to the benefit of the house itself.

Construction: Jorge Romero
Decoration: María del Carmen Rodríguez Franco

Villa Toranzo
MADRID, SPAIN **1974**

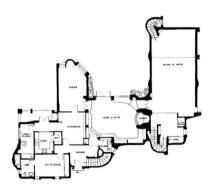

Villa Toranzo, located in the La Moraleja housing development of Madrid, was projected for Fernando Calderón—mountain artist, a cousin and friend of mine—taking into account his atelier, which needed high doors where large-sized paintings could go in and out, because of the almost muralistic scañe in which he expressed his extraordinary talent. Right next to the atelier were to be the living quarters for Marly, his wife, and his four children, as well as Angeles, the nanny, and all sorts of pets, among which, of course, the dogs.

The house was to be an "island" which one would seldom feel like leaving because of its comfort and coziness. Fernando was perhaps timid down-deep and liked to take refuge in his imaginative desperation. Art critic Raúl Chávarri, in his book on Fernando Calderón, *El tornaviaje*, said of him that his life was a chimera of strange, tremendously undisciplined mysticism.

It might be said that the relationship of friendship and sincere affection uniting us during those years, due to our frequent travel to Spain, as well as theirs to Mexico, led us to establish a new architect-client relationship: a total absence of economic interests between us, thereby resolving an interesting transaction of our creative worlds. I would give him an architecture for him and his and he would give me, in exchange, from his own world, an interpretation as a painter of us.

Years have gone by since that covenant. His house was built by the Spanish architect Pilo Fernández de Aguilar and I have a beautiful painting of unhurried and clean strokes in my home. In *lejanista* fashion, it represents my family in an unreal rest stop on the trail settling America's Far West. On their side and forming a inseparable part of the group is the old wagon worn out by the trail dust, shovels and skillets. Authentic chimera of timelessness!

I did the project for the house, taking into account the needs of his family, as he likewise did, he on the canvas and I in the spaces. And, except for the habitual regulatory norms and urban provisions of that place, I had the freedom I have always wanted and have almost always obtained in my projects: expressing my dreams and nostalgia.

Villa Mac-Be
ATLIXCO, PUEBLA   1976-1977

The natural spot for the inhabitants of the city of Puebla to spend weekends is the beautiful colonial town of Atlixco, 30 km away. In this short stretch, the temperate climate of the plateau changes to a semi-tropical one of the lowlands, where gardens flower all year around.

In 1976, here in Atlixco, my uncle, Miguel Díaz Barriga and his wife Tere García Carral asked architect Ezquerra, whom they knew because he had lived in Puebla as a youth, for a project for a house and I had the privilege of supervising the work.

During the execution, I learned two things. First, that only with a system of constructive systems, such as those being implemented by architect Ezquerra at his office, can one build so detailed a work with precision, quality and speed, since the ordinary construction worker is not used to this type of work. Second, that this type of architecture does not transmute forms from the past, but becomes satiated with atavisms so as to create a deeply human architecture.

Mac-be was the name my relatives gave to their house, which in Mayan language means "white way" (*sac be*).

Architect Miguel Díaz Barriga

Villa Fernández-Martínez
MONTERREY, NUEVO LEÓN   **1977**

It is always pleasant to talk with José Luis Ezquerra. We do not talk often, but when we see each other, we do so with a lot of affection. We got to be good friends and a good friend is worth more than anything else. I did not know that this time we talked he was going to ask me to do something that sounded easy: "Tell me what it has been like to live in your house." I sit down to put it in words on a piece of paper and I find it is like describing the sentiments evoked listening to a little music, because it is senseless to describe music in words.

Living in our house has been an adventure, like discovering a new city, in which, one day, you find a new store selling music or a café serving some rolls in the afternoon that you would never have imagined. At the beginning, just having moved, it was an adventure to eat dinner on the outside terrace, in front of the living room. Then we discovered the interior patio which, because it was closed off and because of the dimensions it has, produces a sensation of "being in a bedroom," despite being outdoors and having the sky for a ceiling. Then came the discovery of the back patio. which looks out on an oak forest. When we got there, they were sad and listless, but now they are beautiful and robust. To sit down under them on a Sunday afternoon to savor talking with our grown children, perhaps accompanied by a good Havana cigar. This is the corner which we never would have imagined we would sit to enjoy such pleasant hours, sharing with our family. And so, over time, we discovered another six very special places.

In this house, we raised our family: three boys and a girl, who are now grown-up. It has been our faithful companion and silent witness of the most transcendent task of our lives.

Alberto and Roberta Fernández
Construction: Eduardo Padilla Martínez Negrete

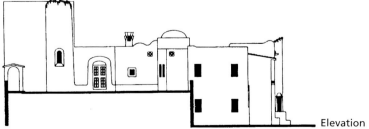

Elevation

Villas Albanas

HORSESHOE BAY, TEXAS **1980**

At the beginning of the eighties, I had the opportunity to delve into what I have called my "North American experience." In the state of Texas, I did a project for a complex of 25 townhouses with a pool and clubhouse on a 1.7 acre piece of land with stupendous views and in front of a golf course designed by Robert Trent Jones.

The spot is surrounded by beautiful landscape, well cared for and protected, where dozens of deer live peacefully around the houses.

One of our greatest challenges was that of building arches and vaults. When we finally resolved it, it was also one of our greatest achievements. We exported Mexican technology, contracting Mexican vault makers, who built some precious vaults with brick (also exported from Mexico), done with the craftsmanship of the old-time vault-maker guilds. Whoever had the opportunity to watch them was strongly impressed by how they erected those cupolas, without any type of framing or formwork. What is most surprising is that the cost of such marvelous work was extremely reasonable.

María Pía Ezquerra
in Villas Albanas
Painting by J.L.. Ezquerra

Color drawings of villas

All these experiences were to be of great use to me some years later, when I was in charge of projecting a huge hotel on the island of Maui in Hawaii. I was familiar with the construction systems and technical languages used in the U.S. and, more specifically, with those directly related with my lejanista architecture.

The *lejanista* evocations of this project, built only in part of what was planed, were expressed unedited by an unknown poet who set down his impressions on the architecture of the villas in *Texas Homes* magazine.

"The exceptional architecture of Villas Albanas come from the ancient traditions, such as the craftsmanship that remains in the construction of brick vaults, a technique handed down from generation to generation since the Middle Ages.

Arches of three and a half points, Isabeline arches, cupolas and niches humanize the interior spaces. Soft and serene stucco encompasses it all, conferring the magic of unexpected surrealism on the claire de lune.

One could say that it has the Spanish influence of the 'legendary Texas' of the XVII and XVIII centuries, although the gothic spirit of the powerful German migration of the XIX century is obvious in the somber and elegant verticalities of the towering chimneys."

Painting of a boy in the villas

Painting of María Luz and Juan
Carlos Ezquerra in Villas Albanas
by J.L. Ezquerra

Villa de Cartes
HORSESHOE BAY, TEXAS ¹⁹⁸⁰

Villa de Cartes, designed for my friends Tere and Emilio Lazagorta as a vacation house, is in the same area and has the same construction and design characteristics as the Villas Albanas project.

It was planed on a single-family lot facing the lake and golf course, on approximately a half acre, with three bedrooms, living room, dining room, kitchen, ample garage space and, of course, a pool and game area.

The peculiarities of this project were the use of brick vaults, the parapet of the entrance tower—representing a pinnacle made with deer antlers and armadillos, animals quite common in the region—and the shaped quarry stone brought from Mexico.

Construction: Architect Leonardo Borobia Souza

Villa Mare Nostrum
CUERNAVACA, MORELOS 1987

In the place in which affection for the land is born, incubates, in childhood, the customs, traditions and all those elements making up the identity of persons, concepts undoubtedly lying within me too, having been born in the Mediterranean, in Barcelona, Spain, emigrated to Mexico to marry and form a family with two different identities, my husband and I were in search of forming, in the home, something would signify the two identities.

So that, during a trip along the Mexican coast, we found what we were looking for in Manzanillo. Our point of union would be the architecture and the work of master architect José Luis Ezquerra.

It met all the requisites: Mediterranean architecture with its own personality, which would help us teach that family integration to our children through the fusion of two cultures, the Mediterranean and the Mexican. The moderateness of Mediterranean culture, a consequence of the passage or influence of many cultures and the exotic, at least in the vegetation of the Mexican atmosphere.

An so Mare Nostrum was born. A private home developed on five thousand square meters of land, which was chosen by the architect himself in light of different options which had been presented to us, and on which it was incredible to see the naturalness of the development of architect Ezquerra´s architectural project. In three or four chats, he had understood the importance for our family of his designing the house and why this would mean, to us, respecting Mediterranean architecture and Mexican vegetation.

Today, fourteen years after its construction, "Mare Nostrum" means the daily encounter with identity, the appreciation of the beauty of the curves and the whiteness, and the feel of being close to the Mediterranean, uniting with Mexico through the design of the garden with the generosity of the foliage. Due to Cuernavaca`s climate, it is formed by all the bushes and plants sown in a garden, always respecting the architecture, which is the soul of this habitat.

This reminds us constantly of the two cultures joining the two axes of the Salgado Berengueras family. We perceive that our children have identified, with precision, part of the sociological elements of the identity of their parents, making a fusion of the undissolvable ties between their habitat and their roots.

All this is what the architectural work of architect José Luis Ezquerra means for me. We have to applaud his commitment not to separate his European roots, always maintaining an architecture of tradition and of vanguard, which, at the same time, is forming a new school that permits us to enjoy the beauty of creativity.

Owner: María Elena Berengueras Sánchez
Construction and expansion: Architect José Luis Mendoza Orozco

Villa Salamandra
NUEVO VALLARTA, NAYARIT 1987

Villa Salamandra has a southwestern face, a basic axis in its general composition between land and sea, and is built on a terrain of approximately 3,300 square meters, with almost 60 square meters along the beachfront. The terrain, though magnificently landscaped, has a depression after the beach dune, which creates not only a worrisome problem of drainage, but could lead to the house being hidden, without a view and too hot.

The solution of raising up the structure, despite its cost, was authorized by the clients, thanks to a desire to achieve an optimum project. The result was extremely positive, since the house acquired an air and elegance, as if it had been built on a hill, in the same way that the Mayan structures in the jungle rise above the horizon formed by the treetops of the low-lying jungle. Villa Salamandra could then have 360° views and breezes.

This spectacular location meant using roofs to their fullest, enjoying them like stone gardens and terrace-*miradores* to their maximum. Therefore, its richness in the design of shapes, parapets, connecting bridges and stairways, in the style of the geometrism of Vasarely, as can be appreciated in the stairway of the façade facing the sea. It goes from the exterior, penetrating the curved vertical wall of the façade, so as to introduce itself into the interior of the main hall.

Villa Salamandra is a baroque-maritime house, optimistic and delicate. It is feminine because it was made with sensual sensitivity, in a framework of serenity. It has several bedrooms for family and guests, a studio, living room and dining room. The outside recreation and service areas, terraces, passageways and pool were resolved with volumetric and spatial autonomy. Therefore, the complex is the sum of the parts or of the functional individualities. It is a little big world of shapes, which achieve "unity in diversity" among themselves, an esthetic principle which I have always defended.

The *lejanismo* of these forms comes from its "baroque intention," the emotive inspiration of the light, from the "white on white." It comes from the impressionistic recollections of paintings such as *Cosiendo la vela, La siesta* and *El paseo a la orilla del mar* by Joaquín Sorolla, where the painting of white on white, the lights and absences, give the sensation

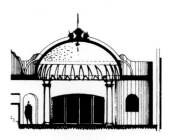

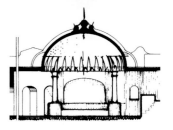

Section: living area

of the warmth of the mornings and summertime evenings on the beaches of Valencia. These emotions have made me think that beach architecture, so committed to temperature, could express, in different ways, the impression of the skin recalled in terms of heat.

These emotions, announced through paintings—I cite only two of my favorites: Joaquín Sorolla and Claude Monet (El paseo del acantilado, Los témpanos, and The Portico of the Cathedral of Rouen)—inspired me to project those attractions for light in beach architecture, as if they were paintbrush strokes, heavy with paint.

Villa Salamandra was a project in which I had these sentiments and stimuli, which were not only supported, but also requested, by the owners themselves.

Construction: *Architect Francisco Montalvo*
Decoration: *Victoria Ezquerra de Lascurain*
Owners: *Rubén and Louise Mereles*

Elevation

Villa del Rocio
SAN ANTONIO, TEXAS **1997**

As time goes by, I am all the more convinced that contacting architect José Luis Ezquerra to project and build our vacation house in San Antonio, Texas, was the best decision. He chose the right spot, a piece of land surrounded by green areas and different levels that allowed us a view of the hills, golf course and trees from the back terrace of the upper floor.

It was a place where he felt comfortable to develop his ideas, according to the initial conversations we had had regarding what we as a family expected from the house. It was easy to coordinate with him. I thoroughly enjoyed the whole process, since the idea was to create a place where we would spend the best moments together as a family, as well as his quality of complementing atmospheres unexpected by us with his designs and original details.

Our home is elegant and, at the same time, informal, as can be seen in the living-room/dining-room and kitchen area, connected to the exterior by the terrace. It is ideal for the family togetherness. The idea was also to keep a certain independence of the octagonal master bedroom vis-à-vis the rest of the complementary areas. I point out the perfect harmony between the builder Roberto Kenigstein and the architect Ezquerra. With the furnishings and paintings, we were assured of confirming its style and achieving that cozy atmosphere which the entire house has and in which we have spent some very pleasant moments.

The owner

I had a privilege and pleasure to build a home designed by Architect Ezquerra in San Antonio, Texas. During construction and later during travels with architect Ezquerra to Morocco and southern Spain, I learned the depth of architect Ezquerra's vision to maintain historical integrity as a part of his architecture. His attention to detail and vast knowledge combine to make his designs timeless.

Construction: Roberto Kenigstein

Villa Antonella
SAN ANTONIO, TEXAS **1999**

José Luis:

The project for our house in San Antonio, Texas has been very satisfying.

It has given us the opportunity to live through your human, very professional and also affectionate ways.

You are, have been and will always be for us a dear and excellent friend.

Elsa and Tony

Owners: Elsa Magnon de Contreras
Antonio Contreras Pages

Villas Pallatium
SAN ANTONIO, TEXAS **1997**

The invitation to write about our home in San Antonio, Texas designed by José Luis Ezquerra, my professor of composition in the 60s at the School of Architecture, Universidad Iberoamericana, is an opportunity to speak, not only as a client, but also as an architect

Villas Pallatium is an ensemble of 79 units in a softly undulating hill covered by a grove of oaks. The site is North of San Antonio, with neighboring commercial lots, religious spaces and other housing developments in a "soft" urban landscape.

It is clear that the intention of Pallatium is to develop spaces of a different Mediterranean style, not yet finished. However, the elements of construction such as walls, doors, windows, arches, roads, patios, gardens with lovely pathways and trails are clear in their message of urban intention. The tower and seven homes clearly show the architectural proposal of Ezquerra.

Architect Guillermo Casas Pérez
Owner

Color drawing of
clubhouse by J.L. Ezquerra

Villa Clara

BOSQUES DE LAS LOMAS 1986

José Luis Architecture has silently become part of our life. Living within his architectural concepts of light and space has enhanced our sense of clarity, grandeur and harmony. The white walls and uncomplicated styles symbolize the simplicity of the life we would like to lead, not always possible with seven boys!

In light is understood as the reflection of God´s creation, and space as the reflection of his greatness, then the fusion of the two is harmony. Often, when I am walking downstairs to the kitchen, as I come across the open area of the sitting room, I feel a surge deep inside me as I contemplate for a moment the beauty of the play between light and space, the thick white walls thrusting up towards the high ceiling, the light flowing in from behind the arch and I stop to consider the blessing of our home.

Jesus and Marie Claire Hernandez
Owners

Villa Casanueva
MEXICO CITY 1994

This is a residence on the outskirts of the city. There were three children, two twins and a little baby, all charming, and their parents always did everything multiplied by three. They planted three trees, made three paths and placed three rocks in the garden. They will always be alive in the capital of the portico of the house, because they are expressed in the carved stone.

This villa, given the quality and lejanista circumstances of its owners, Magala and Guillermo Casanueva de la Colina, will remain full of maritime and luminous nostalgia, especially on certain spaces where their "homesickness" has been trapped.

Villas Lugo

LA HERRADURA 1983
LOMAS COUNTRY CLUB 1996

José Luis

It has been a beautiful experience. My family and I have been not only satisfied, but happy and comfortable all these years, as owners of the homes you have designed for us.

There is so much I would like to express about the wonderful moments of the past when "you and my family" enjoyed together from start to finish our dreams for a living space. I would joyfully journey with you new moments of excitement and expectations.

I admired your ease at drawing: "the fastest hand around," "la mano de Pepe." Maybe, a proper and quicker way to give you our feelings, is to say, ¡OLE! But I would like to add some short and quick words about these homes:

La Herradura
Lovely Mediterranean home, full of light and arches

Acapulco
Beautiful Moorish garden, kept up today beautifully. Inviting space, with a nice swimming pool.

Interior views in La Herradura

Villa Lugo in the Lomas Country Club

Front door of La Herradura

Villa Lugo in the Lomas Country Club

Lomas Country Club, Mexico City

Different, but very Ezquerra, and also very functional.

You are so right when you say that "spaces educate," but not only that. In these homes, we have sensed feelings and emotions, perhaps your connections with other times.

Distinction, character and personality in architecture. I guess that's you. I look forward to new and pleasant moments for future projects.

Federico G. Lugo Molina

Interior view of Lomas Country Club

One of the primary reasons we decided to build a home in México... even though we are Brazilian..., was because of the opportunity to have it designed and built by José Luis Ezquerra. At the time we were renting a home he had designed, and we felt in love with both the beauty of his design as well as the feeling it gave us... "aconchegante" in Portuguese.

You just feel like you're home, even if home is, as with us, thousands of miles away. Living in an Ezquerra home is unique you're surrounded by extraordinary, espectacular architecture, as is our home, but at the same time, you feel warmth and peace. Very much like the man himself.

David and Ana Palfenier

Lomas Country Club golf course

Villas Amalia

BOSQUES, MEXICO CITY **1984**
SANTA FE, MEXICO CITY **1999**

A few years ago, we decided to build our main residence in Mexico City and set out our aims and objectives to achieve a design which would reflect the lifestyle of our family within the warmth and elegance of a Tuscan villa. The site for the home was located in a small wooded valley known as Bosques de las Lomas. Our choice of architect was not difficult. We had known José Luis Ezquerra for several years through his many works in Mexico and elsewere in the world. He is an architect of international repute, who really was able to interpret our inspirations and translate them in terms of form, space, volume and texture. In the hands of this master, a home was built of great character and elegance: a wonderful living place for our family.

Our most recent project is a house located on a hilly site in Santa Fe (Mexico City), with spectacular views which José Luis has exploited to the maximum. His sculptural appreciation is manifest in this building, within which he has created a design perfectly satisfying the multi-faceted aspirations of our family.

Over the years, we have developed a cherished friendship based on genuine respect and admiration. Our sincere thanks, José Luis!

The owner

1984: Bosques neighborhood,
with its charming entranceway

1999: Santa Fe area, full of class and charm,
notwithstanding its urban limitations

Adham Residence
JEDDAH, SAUDI ARABIA 1997

We were honored by His Excellency Sheik Kamal Adham asking us to design his new residence in Jeddah, in association with my friend, architect Nasser Al Jawhary.

Throughout the design process, we enjoyed several meetings with His Excellency.

We thank him again for this opportunity.

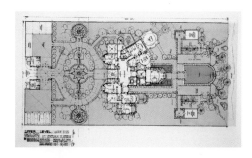

Architecture and Friendship

Architecture and friendship has united José Luis Ezquerra and myself. We have enjoyed long conversations in Mexico, Atlanta and El Cairo about architecture and its philosophy.

Bill Laubmann brought us together for the master plan of Berenice on the Red Sea.

We were honored by Sheik Kamal Adham asking us to design a house in Jeddah for him.

José Luis and I shared our feelings and emotions about producing a project depicting contemporary Islamic architecture. Three very important cultural roots were incorporated in our design: the Middle East, Spain and Mexico.

We had a very enjoyable meeting at the Laubmann house in Atlanta. After a wonderful lunch, we spent the evening discussing Mimar Sinan Abdulmenan, the wonderful architect of the Ottoman culture.

Thank you, Sheik Kamal Adham. Thank you, Bill Laubmann, of Laubmann & Reed Associates. And thank you, José Luis, for being my friend and work partner.

Architect: Nasser Al Jawhary
Palace Constructor

Preliminary Skecth

Mañanitas Casanueva
CUERNAVACA, MORELOS **1994**

I want to express my great admiration and respect for José Luis Ezquerra. He has capacity to capture the needs and desires of his clients and transforms those dreams into reality.

We wanted to create an ambiance of enclosure and, at the same time, give a feeling of open space. We needed a covered drive-through area, followed by a large parking area, unseen by arriving guests. Our reception area had to welcome guests onto a large garden, ending in a pond fed by a waterfall.

His vision enables him to capture his clients ideas and put them on paper. Having heard what our needs were and, with pen in hand, he made a few notations. Soon afterward, he presented us with a project that we loved at first sight.

His genuine love and interest in creating are felt most thoroughly the more you get to know him. He is a talented architect who is able to deal with dreams without losing his ability to construct reality. You can tell that he loves what he does just by watching him create. Something he is able to do because he has a loving family and many friends and satisfied clients who admire his sense of being both an architect and a man.

Rubén Cerda Valladolid
President and CEO
"Las Mañanitas"

Catholic-Byzantine
Cathedral of Parma
CLEVELAND, OHIO **1979**

The Bishop of Parma, His Excellency Emil J. Mihalik, thinks that my architecture has a major Byzantine tendency, so that he entrusted me to make the project for his cathedral. Due to the fact his rites are Byzantine, in all his parishes, allusion is made to the formal similarities with the onion cupolas of Central Europe and to the iconostases of gold tiles and, of course, to the images of Hagia-Sophia, Saint Helen of Constantinople, etc. (Istanbul, Turkey).

In my *lejanista* nostalgia, I turned to the examples of architect Sinan, the "Magnificent," author of so many marvelous works that lent an unforgettable personality to the Ottoman Empire, as well as to the spectacular Saint Sophia, by Anthemius of Tralles. I illustrate this project with sketches, floor plans and perspectives.

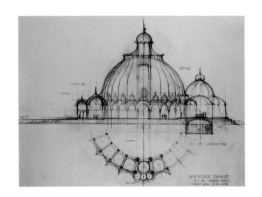

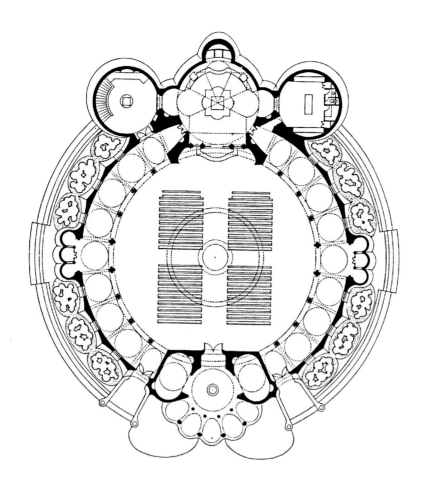

Virgo Fidelis Chapel
CHIPILO, PUEBLA 1995

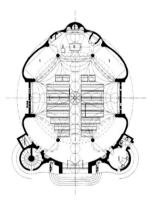

The project for the Convent of the Virgo Fidelis Sisters, a congregation founded a few years ago by the R.P. José Pereda Crespo, founder, in turn, of the Crusades of Christ King. It was projected by José Luis Ezquerra on a hillside in Chipilo, Puebla. It is ennobled by an impressive view of the volcanoes and the Valley of Cholula.

The center of the project is the chapel with an octagonal floor plan, inspired in the forms of Marian femininity. It has two lateral towers, one of them, the one on the right, is simulated, a type of pigeon loft, topping off the cupola of the baptistery. The other leads, by a spiral staircase, to the bell tower, the belfry, whose moldings and shapes paint this façade with stunning and stirring lights and shadows as the sun moves about.

This octagonal chapel is covered with a circular vault held up by eight slender columns, like stalks topped by capitals opening up like bunches of leaves, thereby expressing the Resurrection *(anastasis)*.

On the main façade, topped off axially by the belfry, one infers the Trinitarian Order, in a virtual composition of an isosceles triangle, in whose upper vertex is a *pietà* descending from the cross and, in the two opposite angles, the presence of the doctors of the Church: Saint Theresa of Avila and Saint Catalina of Siena.

In the middle of the vault, a skylight illuminates the pattern formed by varying colors and textures of quarry stone. This light and the white paint of the chapel produce a special mysticism and fascination.

On the sides of the chapel are two buildings of cells-rooms for the sisters, designed with a desk and a bed, as well as a place for meditation in the window, where they can contemplate the landscape.

In the front of the chapel, a classroom and workshop building complement the project, forming a medieval cloister that reminds us of the Cistercian Middle Age of Saint Bernard.

Separated from this complex and united by a vaulted passageway are the services: dining rooms, kitchen, laundry room, etc., utilizing the different level of the terrain.

The structure of all the buildings is based on load walls, always taking into account the seismic nature of the area, which makes them very stable.

Because of its philosophy, this project seems to me one of José Luis Ezquerra's best and I feel quite satisfied to have been able to collaborate with him on this work.

Architect Gabriel Gómez Castillo

The project for the convent-lodging of the Society of the Apostolic Life of Virgo Fidelis in Chipilo, Puebla was conceived based on the reform set down by Saint Bernard of Clairvaux in the XII century. Its principles are: Illumination, Rigor, Creation and Heritage. The society is interested in regulating the construction of the convents of its order, giving them a character of their own based on the esthetics of art, but adapting, in turn, to the teachings and principles handed down by Saint Benito in the liturgy, sacred chant, etc...and to all the philosophy of monastic life.

Therefore, the purpose of this project was to revive this tradition, establishing the artistic and architectural norms of the foundation, giving personality to style, shapes and spaces to the constructions of the societies of the Crusades of Christ King and Virgo Fidelis. Therefore, they hope to attain that the imprint of the Religious Family is clear, that is, that, seeing the different works, it is evident that they belong to it.

However, it is the utmost importance not to be repetitive, to not "copy" the projects of one building to another, but rather to make the prototype a principle or fundamental spurring the spirit of creativity, taking advantage of the inexhaustible possibilities of the works of creation.

Some of the concepts from the teachings of Saint Bernard of Clairvaux are, first of all, the elimination of all sumptuous and excessive ornamentation that distracts Man from prayer and interiorization. These ornaments are replaced mainly by light, which should bathe the different spaces of the convent, especially that of the chapel.

We, likewise enthusiastic admirers of baroque art, represented quite specially in the regions near Chipilo, inherited this concept with special interest. We wanted this to be one of the norms governing the construction of this and future works of the convents of Virgo Fidelis and the Crusades of Christ King.

Other concepts used in this project are, for example, the major use of a single material and color in the construction of the different buildings; the predominance of simple octagonal forms in the floor plans and volumes of the project; the incorporation of artisan materials and work from the region, such as stucco, gold leaf, brick, tile, colored jars and other crafts which are abundant in the valleys of Cholula and Puebla; and, finally, the search to stamp the femininity of Mary on the convents of Virgo Fidelis. That femininity is immersed, for example, in the Capilla del Rosario in Puebla.

Finally, it is of vital importance for this lodging to assure its functions are adequate at all times for the human being that lives praying and working *(ora et labora)* in this space of life and spirituality.

Color elevation

Calzada de los
VILLA DE GUADALUPE, MEXICO CITY

The criterion we applied, supported by the Letter of Venice for the artistic and historical rescue of the monuments to which we refer, was based on directing and unveiling the esthetic and historical values of the monuments with regard to their own ancient values and the use of authentic documents for decision-making regarding the restoration schedule and process that was used.

In general terms, the work included an integral plan of exploration for each one of the monuments and its surroundings, based on a painstaking analysis and research of both the architectural as well as the iconographic components, from which came the thesis of the origins of the fabrication of each one of them, as well as the study of its historical profile.

Carrying out the executive restoration project encompassed historical research in archives and libraries, as well as field research, which was of vital importance, since it generated information and data that were only mentioned in some of the documents reviewed. Example: the information mentioned by Fray Juan de Torquemada in 1604, in which he related the original measurements for the first time. Another piece of information was provided by Fray Francisco de Ajofrin, a Benedictine friar who, in a visit to New Spain in the XVIII century (1757), confirmed in his *Relación del viaje a América* the same data provided by Fray Juan de Torquemada some one hundred and fifty years earlier. Similarly, once the information from the documents was verified and gone over with that from the field research, we were satisfied to have found the vestiges that confirmed the reports of the documents by the aforementioned friars.

It is also important to mention our experiences in being able to rescue the vestiges found in the cracks of the stone ornaments, sheets of lime with layers of color in different stratigraphy, which allowed us to do an analysis of colors and propose their use on plastered surfaces and quarry stone. This could be done once the palette of colors was confirmed, provided to us by a prior chemical and stratigraphic study of the presence of polychromy existing in the moments still standing.

Therefore, the rechromatization of the monuments was decided. We should explain that the use of bare quarry stone without any

Third Sorrowful Mystery
"Coronation of Thorms"

Design by Victoria Ezquerra

Misterios

Urban-Architectural Restoration   **1997 - 1998**

Drawing by J.L. Ezquerra

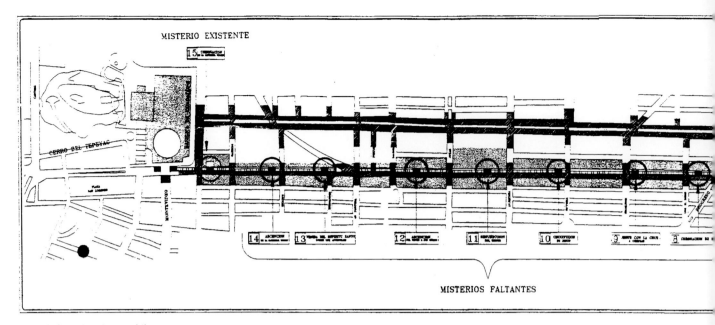

Calzada de los Misterios: 4.5 kilometers

Application of color or protection was a fashion that began in the second half of the XIX century in France and that continues on until our days. However, this criterion was not common in the centuries of Mexican baroque, in which stone was normally polychromatic.

Mysteries, Religion and Art
DEVOTION TO THE VIRGIN

In contrast to other forms of Christianity, Catholics are known for the importance they concede to the figure of the Virgin as the Mother of God. This importance is expressed in dedications, devotions and different prayers, outstanding among which is the devotion to the rosary and its prayers. They center on fifteen episodes from the life of the Virgin, known as the *misterios* (mysteries). There are three types of episodes: joyful, sorrowful and glorious.

The monuments lining the causeway were built on the model set down by the first one, as designed by master architect Cristóbal de Medina Vargas. They are clear examples of the New Spanish baroque art. Differences between one monument and another are solely in the ornamentation and in the central theme. The latter represents an episode, or mystery, and the direction and order of their placement corresponds to pilgrims' route from Mexico City to the sanctuary of the Virgin of Guadalupe.

Architect: Fernando A. Sánchez Chávez

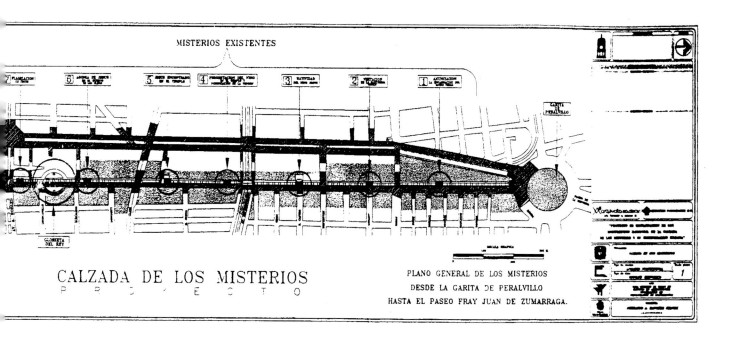

MISTERIOS EXISTENTES

CALZADA DE LOS MISTERIOS
P R O Y E C T O

PLANO GENERAL DE LOS MISTERIOS
DESDE LA GARITA DE PERALVILLO
HASTA EL PASEO FRAY JUAN DE ZUMARRAGA.

SECOND JOYFUL MYSTERY
VISIT OF HOLY MARY
TO HER COUSIN, SAINT ISABEL

SECOND JOYFUL MYSTERY (Restored)
VISIT OF HOLY MARY
TO HER COUSIN, SAINT ISABEL

WORKS AND PROJECTS
UNDERWAY SINCE 1997

Amphitrite Palace Hotel
SKHIRAT, MOROCCO **1998 – 2000**

It is an honor and a quite serious commitment for us to collaborate in the creation of this maritime palace of Skhirat and to achieve a beauty of excellence.

Its magnificent location, right next to the Royal Beach Palace, obligates us to give the best of our capacities as architects so as to achieve a work of utmost taste and style. Thus, the importance for us of the axes of visual composition when structuring the "hotel-palace" complex elegantly and grandly.

For that very same reason, we have chosen a solution which, surrounded by gardens, permits obtaining the best views, not only for the majority of rooms and apartments, but also visual freedom for the public areas.

One of them, constituting the core of the project, is the plaza of the "Half Moon," with its fountains and peripheral galleries.

The delicate touch and good taste, the search for esthetics, and the sensuality of its forms and spaces are presents for the spirit of its visitors.

The Amphitrite Palace Hotel project is a project for good living, with life in movement, with poetry and nostalgia, with sweetness and beauty, all rooted in the

The architect on site

Preliminary sketches

site and respecting its history and its culture.

The architecture is white and pure, so that the brilliance of its ivory-tone roofs and the colors of its flowers and gardens, will be exhalted!

Nature, water and light represent paradise for Man…sunlight can wander the surface of the architectural forms from sun-up to sun-down, without gaps or obstacles, in a constant shifting of effects and of chromatic contrasts, quite suggestive for visitors.

We hope that our project produces an enjoyable emotional clash in them and that our Amphitrite Palace Hotel grants pleasures and emotions to their spirit, rendering it unforgettable.

Architects: Omar Alaoui, Karim Chakor
Owner: Britannic Hotels

Preliminary Sketches

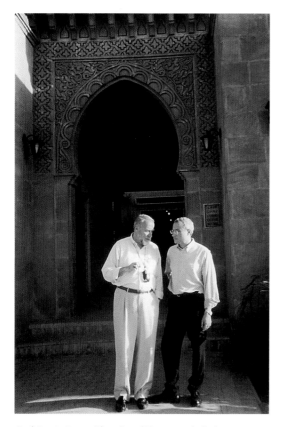

Architects Omar Alaoui and Ezquerra in Rabat

Berenice
RED SEA, EGYPT   **PROJECT UNDERWAY**

We were invited by the firm Laubmann & Reed Associates, based in Atlanta, Georgia, to join the architectural team working with the group of Saudi High Excellency Sheik Kamal Adham on the formidable 200,000-person mega-resort that is planed to be built on the Ptolemaic peninsula of Berenice, on the Red Sea some 250 km from Gamal Abdel Nasser lake, close to the Sudanese border and to the cities on the opposite bank: Jeddah and Mecca, in Saudi Arabia.

We were assigned one of the two development poles to provide an image and a modern Islamic style. We are currently working on this and some initial concepts have been contributed.

But this project, perhaps provincial, may have a more transcendental meaning in my professional life. At the beginning of this book, I spoke of our 1961 trip to Egypt with the group from the History Seminar at the UNAM. The purpose was to cooperate in rescuing the Egyptian temples of the Nubian area, from Philae (Ptolemic) to Abu-Simbel, which were in danger of being buried under the waters of the huge lake produced by the Sadd-el-Ali dam.

The reservoir was named after its promoter, President Gamal Abdel Nasser, who invited us to visit his country as guests of honor. Precisely from this lake, through an incredible engineering project 250 km. long, water will be diverted to the new tourist city of Berenice, on the desert coast of the Red Sea.

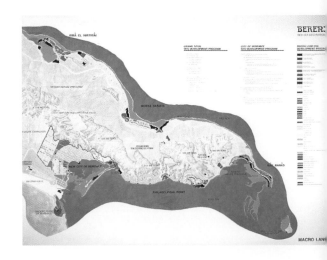

Since that trip, almost forty years of professional work have passed, as is described in this book. At times, I ask myself if this coincidence means something, since I have always believed that everything is written down and nothing moves, not even the leaves on the trees, but by the will of God.

Preliminary sketches

Berenice

Berenice in an international destination, a multi-resort complex and support city located on the Red Sea in Egypt. The site is situated on a peninsula known as Râs Banâs, which forms Foul Bay, the largest and most beautiful protected bay on the Egyptian coast. The location offers spectacular mountain views, excellent protected beaches, world-famous virgin reefs and a pristine desert environment. The site encompasses the ancient ruins of the Ptolemaic city of Berenice, founded in 275 BC, which flourished as a commercial port for over 500 years. Berenice served as the major junction of the trade routes from the Nile Valley, Africa, India, the Near East and Europe.

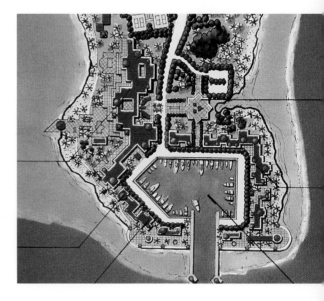

The four-resort development will be built over a 25-year period and will include a total of 10,000 hotel rooms, 2,800 condominium units, 400 apartments, 900 residential villa lots, and commercial and entertainment areas. The amenities include three 18-hole golf courses, three marinas, nine swim/tennis clubs, three equestrian centers, a convention center, a museum next to the ancient ruins of Berenice, health spa, golf and tennis academy, scuba-diving centers, mosques and all related support facilities.

The master plan calls for the new planned city of Berenice, which will have a population of 200,000 inhabitants. There are four separate and distinctive areas, each with its own unique environs and identity. The master planning incorporated a sensitive environmental planning and design approach which developed guidelines that insure the protection of sensitive and valuable site resources, such as reefs, sand dunes, desert and mountain environments and historic sites.

William H. Laubmann
Architect

Râs Banâs

Râs Banâs is a narrow body of land that was formed by calcified coral and is 6.2 km long. Separating Foul Bay from the Red Sea, Râs Banâs has excellent beaches, sheltered water and spectacular views of sunrises over the Red Sea, sunsets over Foul Bay and the distant mountains.

Râs Banâs is envisioned as a five-star destination hotel and residential resort. The guests will enjoy the greatest possible variety of sports, including golf, equestrian, tennis, beach and boating activities. Râs Banâs has a marina village where each house has its separate boa dock, elegant beachfront hotels, condominiums and private villas, a conference center and a corniche with a large beach and a commercial/entertainment village.

The landscape and architecture will reflect a nomadic Moorish village evoking memories of the adventures of the Arabian Nights. The architecture will be white and pure so that the color of plants and flowers will stand out amidst the built edges. The gardens will reflect a "sense of place" that evolved through reflections of culture, climate and landscape.

William H. Laubmann
Architect

Preliminary sketch

Villa Lascurain
STATE OF MEXICO **PROJECT UNDERWAY**

This villa is located in the State of Mexico, on a golf course, where its owners, the Victoria and Miguel Lascurain family, plan to spend long periods of rest.

The place is close to magical Malinalco, where one can still breathe both the memories of the noble Eagle Knights of the Tenochca empire, the last bastion of resistance, as well as the mystic monastic chants from the Mudejar and picturesque patios of its convents.

Drawing by J.L.Ezquerra

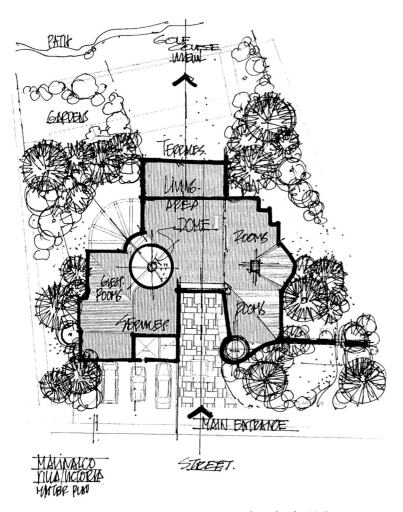

Drawing by J.L.Ezquerra

Drawing by J.L.Ezquerra

Villas Esmeralda
CANCUN, QUINTANA ROO **PROJECT UNDERWAY**

This is a project, currently underway, located in the Paradise Beach development, between Puerto Morelos and Playa del Carmen, some 20 minutes from the airport in the corridor leading to the marvelous and unique Tulum.

We find ourselves before the challenge of giving Villas Esmeralda a character and personality of its own. We visited the cultural antecedents of the peninsula: the marvelous Izamal complex; the bell gables and rooftops of Valladolid; the haciendas and convents on the road between Mérida and Uxmal, such as the Mucuyche Hacienda. The parapets of the churches of Saban, Ichmul and Tabi were some of the interesting points of reference for selecting the shapes and colors we would apply to the project. Special significance was drawn from Tulum and the midget temples of Playa del Carmen, with their humanized, hand-rounded edges and the plastic sensitivity of the ancient Maya.

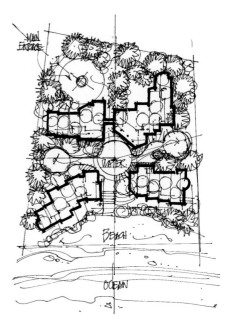

Drawing by J.L.Ezquerra

Drawing by J.L.Ezquerra

Villas Las Almunias
EL TAMARINDO, JALISCO   **PROPOSAL OF AN IMAGE**

1) What is an *almunia*?

An *almunia* is an orchard. It comes from the Mudejar word *almuni,* an "orchard."

2) Why orchards in this project?

Because of the regulatory characteristics of the construction density planed for each lot. No more than 5,000 square meters of the area can be cut down, as well as the same maximum construction surface, with covered areas of no more than 5 levels.

Because of such densities and dimensions for the lots, with regard to the 4 or 5 hectares per lot, one can infer "no easy visual architectural integration" in the landscape, making evident a virtual separation between the different complexes.

However, if all along and "alongside" these communications, obviously done through streets and roadways, we add planted areas (orchards), some extremely attractive links and pleasing shadows can be established (see drawings) from the orchards.

These groves would support the botanical part, with the cultivation of plants, flowers, fruit trees, etc., as well as the ecology of the area, rescuing and encouraging different species.

Should such concept and proposal be possible, it would become a characteristic symbol of the project.

Preliminary sketches

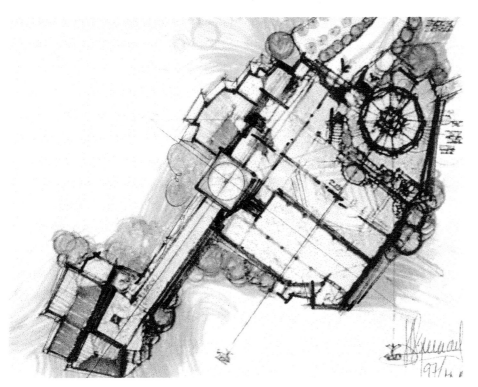

Preliminary sketches

Preliminary sketches

Puerto Mio
ZIHUATANEJO, GUERRERO

Puerto Mío is a nautical-tourist development located in the Grand Bay of Zihuatanejo, on the Pacific coast of Mexico, some 100 miles North of Acapulco and 35 minutes by plane from Mexico City.

On the property, a charming little hotel has been functioning for some years now. It is tucked away in a small, private cove called Puerto Mío, after which the project was named. On the other hand, it is the heart of the peninsula's future development, since it already enjoys well-deserved prestige for its many years of good service and excellent specialties of local Mexican cooking.

The Bay of Zihuatanejo, on the slopes of the Sierra Madre, is a land of history and legends, a place for leisure today, just as it was a sanctuary for Purépecha Indian nobility in times past.

The project contemplates port installations adequate for the mooring of large tourist liners. Consequently, an architectural atmosphere has been planed, inspired in the ancient Mexican coastal peoples, with the particular view of modernity which our friend, architect José Luis Ezquerra, lends to his work.

Héctor Alonso Rebaque
Promoter

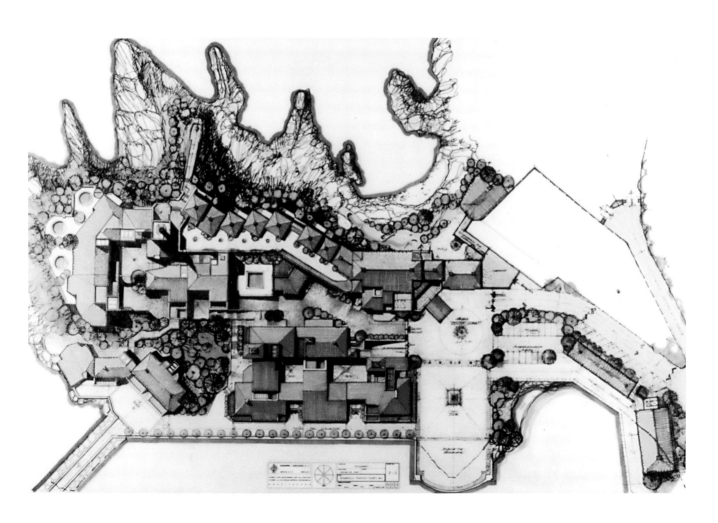

Tehuacán

PUEBLA   URBANISM

Rehabilitating and dignifying urban spaces has always been the ideal dream of urbanists, architects, artists and princes.

The possibility and the imagination of utopias in the humanistic perfection for citizens has not died. On the contrary, in light of the desolating deterioration of the vulgar, pragmatic and uncontrolled growth of our towns and cities, we reconstruct them, undertaking together with their authorities, like modern alchemists, imaginative formulas permitting their rescue, by extracting their real values from their historical and emotional realities.

From the Augustine ideal of a City of God—Saint Benito, Bernard de Clairvaux, Giacomo dei Fiori, Francesq Eixemenis, Arias Montano, Alberti, Vasari, Pedro M. de Angleria and others up to our days—the desire to make cities for the happiness of their citizens has continued in effect. What better way for a good urbanism plan!

We have had the great professional and spiritual pleasure of undertaking and collaborating in urbanistic tasks (of course, underway today) with the mayor of Tehuacán, Felipe Mojarro Arroyo, and his town council. He had understood the transcendence of a good government, through the humanization and dignification of urban surroundings, since, to continue growing in anarchy, is a sure passport to chaos and destruction.

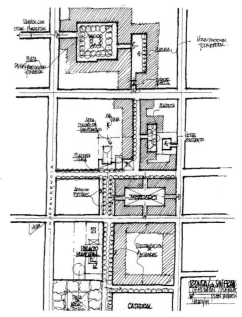

Preliminary sketches

"Carry out the fantasy, defining and measuring everything one can and, with the knowledge of things, achieve power over them."

"Make no little plans; they have no magic to stir men´s blood and probably themselves will not be realized. Make big plans; aim high in hope and work, remembering that a noble, logical diagram once recorded will never die, but long after we are gone will be a living thing, asserting itself with ever-growing insistency. Remember that our sons and grandsons are going to do things that would stagger us. Let your watchword be order and your beacon beauty."

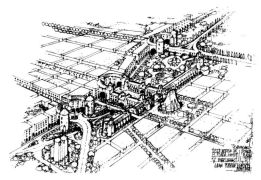

Preliminary sketches

Daniel H. Burnham

Luis Paredes Moctezuma
Professor of Architecture and Urbanism

RONDA DE SAN FRANCISCO
CALLE DEL MERCADO
TEHUACAN. PUEBLA. AGOSTO/1996.

Basilica de Nuestra Señora de los Remedios
NAUCALPAN, STATE OF MEXICO

PROJECT UNDERWAY

This is the first of our topics: the sacred area and the surroundings of the Basilica de Nuestra Señora de los Remedios which, though surrounded by a gigantic urban sprawl, still has good chances of rescue due to the wooded areas surrounding it.

With the experience and the antecedent of the trust of the Basilica de Nuestra Señora de Guadalupe, a noteworthy legal formula to guarantee permanent action in urban improvements and rescue, a group of friends started gettomg together for pleasant chats. The mayor of Naucalpan at that time, José Luis Durán, attended one of them at the beginning. As mayor, he enthusiastically supported the ideals and attractive utopias coming naturally and enthusiastically out of those meetings of architects, historians, artists and businessmen (Ramón Monroy, José Ramón Ortiz, Alvaro Amat, Luis Ortiz Macedo, Fernando Pandal, Francisco Roa, Vivaldo Oregel, Paulina Lascurain, Alfonso Padilla, etc.).

Today, we are planing and working. The generating utopias are becoming realities. Everything is a question of time and perseverance.

Time will be the answer!

Drawing by J.L.Ezquerra

FIDEICOMISO LOS REMEDIOS

MEXICO, 16 DE JUNIO DE 1998   EZQUERRA Y ASOCIADOS, S.C. ARQUITECTOS

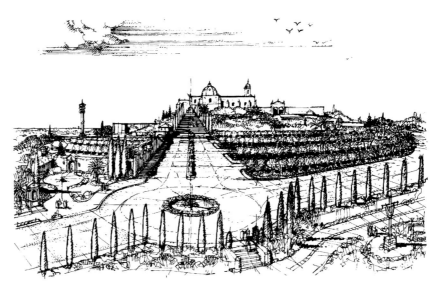

Drawing by J.L.Ezquerra

Drawing by J.L.Ezquerra

International Business Center
OF PUEBLA - CINEP

PROMOTING GROUP:
QUINTANA Y ASOCIADOS
JOSÉ ANTONIO QUINTANA
HERMANOS HUERTA ORTEGA
ARMANDO ORTIZ M.
LUIS PAREDES MOCTEZUMA

The project of the International Business Center of Puebla (CINEP) is the most important the promoting group has undertaken, not only because of its dimensions and characteristics, but also because of its specific weight in the city of Puebla and its region.

For its conceptualization, according to the highest international standards, as well as for its proper location in the socio-cultural and economic context both of the country and of the city, we earmarked major resources to studying similar developments in other parts of the world, such as Germany, Austria, Belgium, Brazil, Colombia, Chile, Spain, the U.S., France, Italy, Panama, Peru, Switzerland, as well as different cities in Mexico, such as Mexico City, Guadalajara, Monterrey, Tijuana, Veracruz and Ciudad Juárez.

Having analyzed the typologies of real-estate developments earmarked primarily for offices and complementary services, its urbanistic and architectural concept was finally located on the outskirts of the city, right at the intersection of the two main urban highways of the region, where there are already modern shopping centers, a golf course, major hotels and other developments, that is, at Atixcayotl and Periférico.

The pilot project defined the areas earmarked for the business center and for housing developments, the basic concept of spaces, and the infrastructure and services to be developed. Prototypes were posited for office buildings, condominiums, villas and residences, which successively passed different market tests, while also defining that our anchor product was the city of Puebla itself, it cultural wealth, its universities, services, businesses, location, climate, etc. which, added to the potential of its macro-region and to the positioning of

RINCON DE LOS REYES

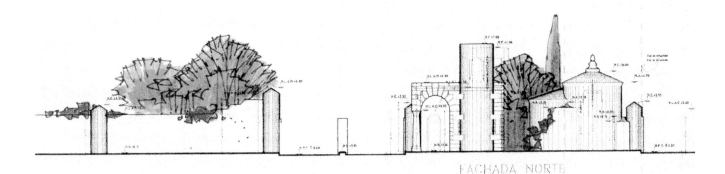

Mexico as a country in function of its commercial agreements (NAFTA, G3, as well as the one currently being negotiated with the European Union), offer us ample perspectives for the investment project.

We were already assured of having a magnificent pilot project, but we wanted something more. Offer the most competitive companies of the country an excellent business center, not only because of its infrastructure and services, but also because of the style and quality of life that would be offered to whomever chooses to do business there and to whomever chooses to live there.

These proposals situated us on another level. We needed someone capable of creating magical atmospheres, so as to have a chance of attracting companies and persons of the highest level worldwide. This would assure us of commercial success and would open up broad perspectives for our future business.

Contacting him and discovering his concepts of art, culture, architecture, sociology and economics, among many other topics we have talked about, reveals a man that is well-rounded, mature, cultivated, analytical and, above all, extraordinarily creative. When studying both our urbanistic and architectural pilot projects, as well as the market probes and other documents, he immediately understood the challenge he was being proposed. Taking the best of our proposal, he did indeed give magic to the development from his very first lines and sketches. He produced strong and impressive volumes which, without being like the typical office buildings we all know, do not deny their function and integrate, together with the insignia hotel, a space which, without repeating those of the historical layout of the city, identify with it and seem to project it to a new and better stage of its existence.

It seemed to us that this architecture he calls *lejanista* is capable of encompassing the people working or going there, as it will also give identity, personality and presence to the companies and corporations setting up there. This will, generate a new neighborhood, modern and characteristic at the same time, for the almost five-time centenary city of Puebla.

José Luis has integrated into our team and has wisely incorporated several of our prototypes into the master plan which we have been maturing together, giving us, in turn, the opportunity to satiate ourselves with his talent and experience, making joint tasks, be they business, architectural, social or cultural, a real pleasure.

Luis E. Paredes Moctezuma
Professor of Architecture and Urbanism

Drawings by J.L. Ezquerra

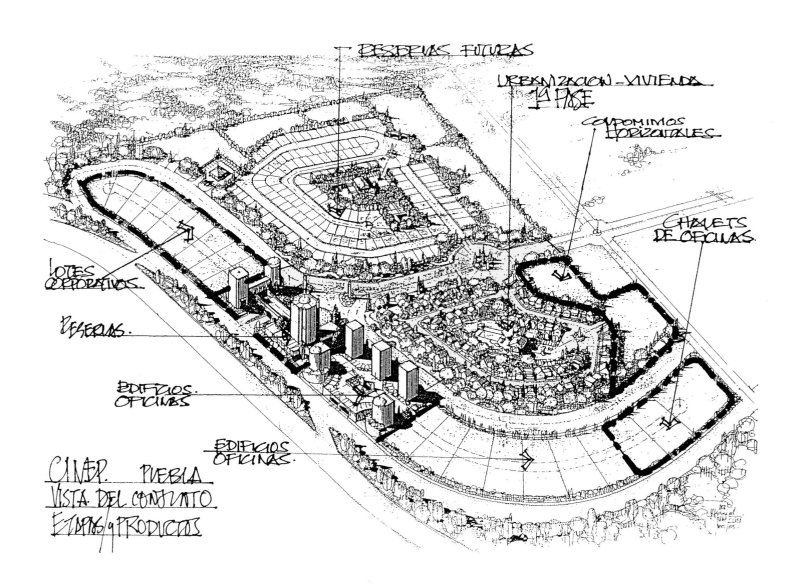

Torre del Molino
LA HERRADURA, STATE OF MEXICO
CONSTRUCTION 1999-2000

By way of an annexed expansion of the residence of María Pia and Francisco Fernández, the Torre de Molino is a tower for recreation and rest, separate from the main house.

A flashback to the straight and vertical nature of the straining and noble windmills which, though "bladeless and windless," provided so many benefits.

Villamalia
ACAPULCO, GUERRERO

The "Villamalia," a small chalet of Tuscan nostalgia, looks out on the sea of no-less nostalgic Acapulco Bay.

Drawings of Acapulco
(Project underway)

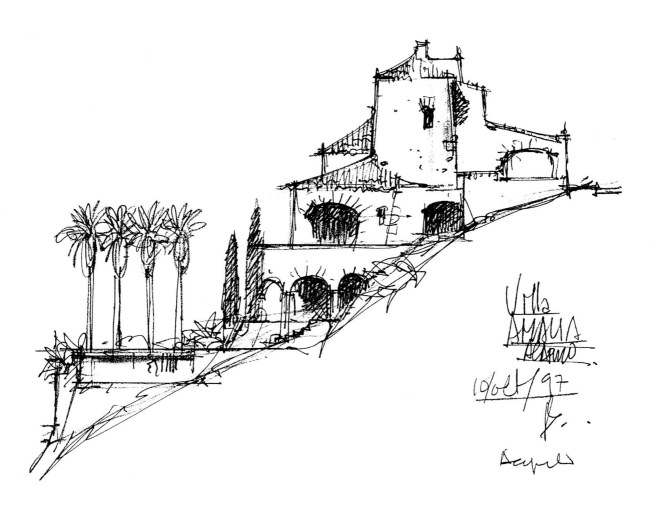

EPILOGUE

Hans Rothlisberger

Once you have read and experienced José Luis Ezquerra's "My Ten Commandments" and "The Tree of My Beliefs," you notice at the same time that his architecture is a feast for the eyes.

I first saw a drawing of Las Hadas in 1973 and decided to come to Mexico to see with my own eyes what was being built. Not only was I enchanted with Mexico and its people, but I fell in love with Las Hadas and its architecture.

After living in one of the towers of Las Hadas for over 20 years, I have had the joy and privilege to meet some of the most interesting people from the entire world. They were all fascinated with what they saw and some came back to build their own mansions above Las Hadas on La Punta, movies like "10" with Bo Derek were shot here, others brought their yachts to this special place and many came to do nothing in style, enjoying the incredible scenery, architecture and peace that Las Hadas evokes.

I also had the great fortune to spend a lot of time with my very talented friend José Luis Ezquerra, travel with him to many destinations in Mexico, Europe and the U.S. to look at new projects and gather new ideas. In all the years we have known each other, we have never stopped talking about future dreams and illusions and I know that "THE BEST IS YET TO COME."

Looking at his present projects like Morocco, Egypt and others and, at the same time, comparing new resorts in the U.S. like the Bellagio and Venezia in Las Vegas or Universal's Portofino in Orlando, I am convinced that José Luis Ezquerra with his ten commandments will be a great part of the new millennium with an explosion of his romantic architecture.

CHRONOLOGY

1.	VILLA LOOSE	1961
2.	VILLA COLOMBA	1961
3.	VILLA VALLADOLID	1962
4.	VILLA MILLARCA	1963
5.	LAS HADAS HOTEL	1964 - 1974
6.	VILLA TORANZO	1974
7.	VILLA MAC – BE	1977
8.	VILLA FERNANDEZ – MARTINEZ	1977
9.	VILLA LA ATALAYA	1977
10.	VILLA COLIMAN	1978
11.	VILLA CORAL	1979
12.	VILLA CASARENA	1979
13.	CLUB MAEVA HOTEL	1979
14.	CLUB MED IXTAPA	1979
15.	TEMPLO CLEVELAND	1979
16.	VILLAS ALBANAS	1980
17.	VILLA DE CARTES	1980
18.	VILLA MARE NOSTRUM	1983
19.	VILLAS LUGO	1983 - 1996
20.	VILLAS AMALIA	1984 - 1999
21.	VILLAS SOLARIS	1985
22.	VILLA CLARA	1986
23.	VILLA LA SALAMANDRA	1987
24.	FALDAS DE LA ALCAZABA	1988
25.	SIERRA MANZANILLO HOTEL	1990
26.	KEA LANI HOTEL	1992
27.	VILLA CASANUEVA	1992
28.	LAS MAÑANITAS – CASANUEVA	1994
29.	VIRGO FIDELIS CONVENT	1995
30.	VILLA JEDDAH	1997
31.	VILLA DEL ROCIO	1997
32.	VILLAS PALLATIUM	1997
33.	CALZADA DE LOS MISTERIOS	1998
34.	VILLA IN LOMAS COUNTRY CLUB	1998
35.	VILLA ANTONELLA	1999

WORKS AND PROJECTS UNDERWAY SINCE 1997

1. AMPHITRITE PALACE HOTEL
2. BERENICE MASTER PLAN
3. VILLA LASCURAIN
4. VILLAS ESMERALDA
5. VILLAS LAS ALUMUNIAS
6. PUERTO MIO MASTER PLAN
7. TEHUACAN MASTER PLAN
8. LOS REMEDIOS MASTER PLAN
9. INTERNATIONAL BUSINESS CENTER OF PUEBLA
10. TORRE DEL MOLINO
11. VILLAMALIA